HELL ON THE DOORSTEP

JOHN AND JAN GRAHAM
WITH
MEREDITH RESCE

Hell on the Doorstep
Meredith Resce, John Graham, Jan Graham
© 2018

All rights reserved. No portion of this book may be used, reproduced or transmitted in any form or by any means digital, electronic, mechanical, photocopy, recording or otherwise without written permission of the authors or publisher except in the case of brief quotations within critical articles and reviews.

Golden Grain Publishing
PO Box 880, Unley, SA, 5061

The National Library of Australia Cataloguing-in-Publication information:

ISBN print book 978-0-9945786-8-6
ISBN eBook 978-0-9945786-9-3

 A catalogue record for this book is available from the National Library of Australia

Scripture quotations marked (NIV) are taken from the Holy Bible, New International Version®, NIV®. Copyright © 1973, 1978, 1984, 2011 by Biblica, Inc.™ Used by permission of Zondervan. All rights reserved worldwide. www.zondervan.com The "NIV" and "New International Version" are trademarks registered in the United States Patent and Trademark Office by Biblica, Inc.™

Christian non-fiction; Biography
Cover Design – Dragan Bilic

I read *Hell on the Doorstep* in one sitting. I found it incredibly moving as the authors shared the devastating tragedy of the Victorian Black Saturday Bushfires – 173 lives lost and numerous families left scarred and broken. I appreciated the vulnerability and frankness in which John and Jan Graham shared their own journey, not just through the immediacy of the tragedy but in the many months afterwards when the smoke and fire had gone. The insight and wisdom they shared provides essential lessons for anyone who finds themselves ministering to those in crisis. The book finishes with a poignant challenge from editor Meredith Resce – that all of us be moved to practical and loving action; that all of us respond with a 'yes' to the mess.

Jon Cathie
Senior Pastor
Capital Edge Community Church, Canberra
Author of *Reflections from Gallipoli*

Hell on the Doorstep is the compelling true story of a couple who lived in the community that suffered through the horrifying ordeal of the Black Saturday Bushfires. I was captured by the raw emotion that John and Jan Graham describe as they tell of their experiences as relief workers. I was inspired by the courage and resilience depicted, that is often found in times of human tragedy. This story of collective support from the community in times of adversity will remind readers that: alone we can do so little, but together, we can do so much.

Pastor Zoran Paunovich
Vice President, Planetshakers College, Melbourne
Author of *In Your Dreams*

I found myself riding a roller coaster of emotions as I read the true-life story of *Hell on the Doorstep*. I felt I walked every step with these incredible people as I listened to the heartache and pain of such horror. Nobody can ever be fully prepared for such a tragedy. *Hell on the Doorstep* gave me a glimpse into the lives of everyday people who are carrying grief and trauma from life's circumstances. But as I read I also sensed hope in the face of hopelessness. There are people who are ready to help in time of great need. This book has given me a greater awareness that the church isn't just a Sunday only thing—church is every day of the week, reaching out and lifting people up from their ashes.

Pastor Nikki Rucci
River City Family Church, Brisbane

Table of Contents

Map of the Fire Ground	vii
Foreword – Meredith Resce	ix
Introduction – John Graham, Jan Graham	1
Chapter One: The Fury is Unleashed	5
Chapter Two: The Shock Sinks In	21
Chapter Three: Emerging From the Chaos	27
Chapter Four: The Food and Clothing Bank	31
Chapter Five: Gone From the Nightly News	39
Chapter Six: I Never Saw This Coming	55
Chapter Seven: Rising From The Ashes	59
Chapter Eight: The Local Community Rises To The Challenge	63
Chapter Nine: Who is My Neighbour?	67
Chapter Ten: How To Become A Part Of The Support Network	73
About the Authors	81

Link to online map:

https://www.ffm.vic.gov.au/__data/assets/pdf_file/0011/20261/Kilmore-EastMurrindindiOverview_20090406.pdf

Acknowledgment:

Contains Vicmap information © The State of Victoria, Department of Environment, Land, Water & Planning, 2018.
   Reproduced by permission of the Department of Environment, Land, Water & Planning.

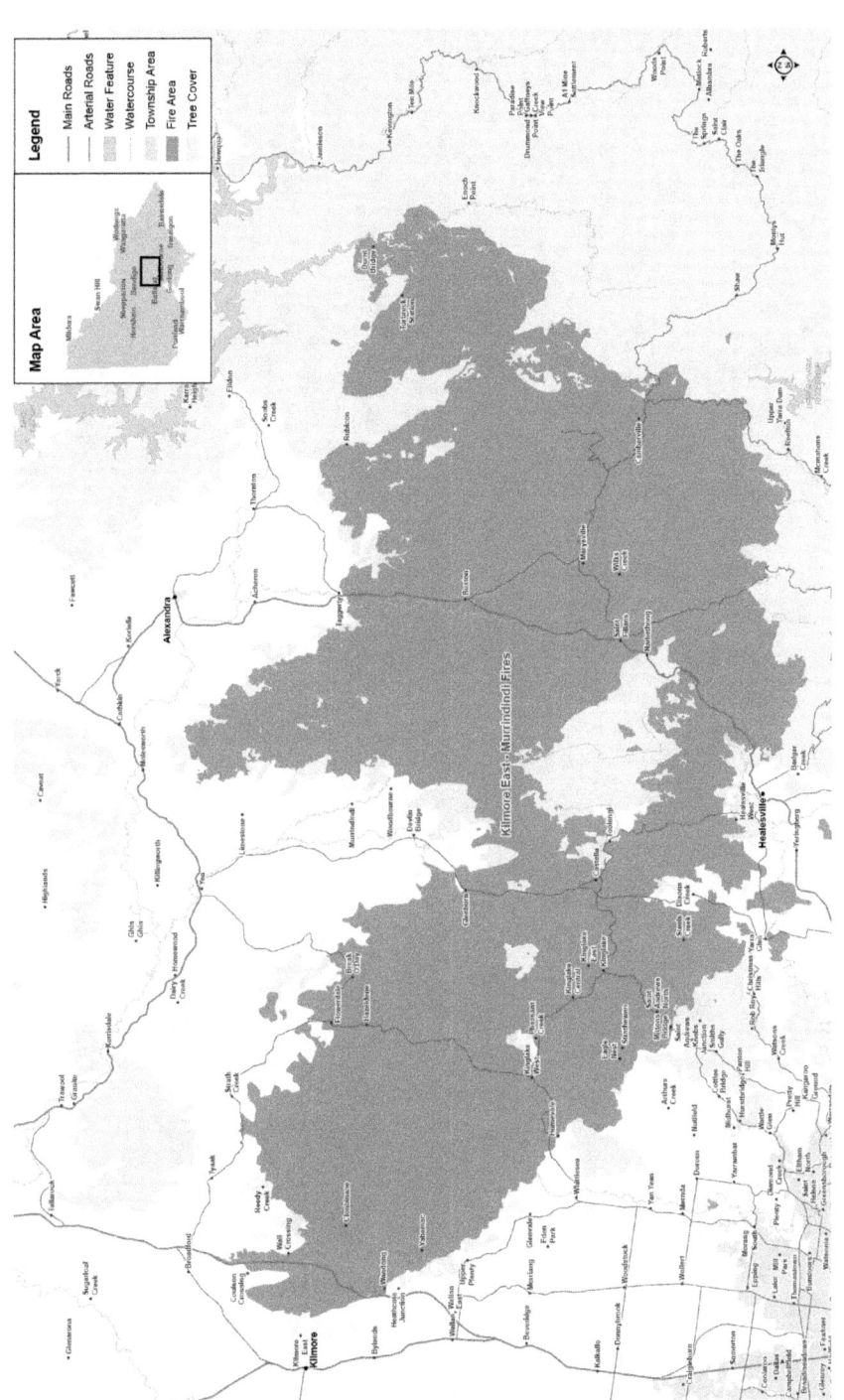

Foreword

My friend, Jan, and I were engaged in a deep and meaningful conversation about the church and our community. We both expressed our frustration knowing there is trouble throughout our society, but often Christians in a nice, cosy church setting rarely see it. One seldom feels prompted to meet a need unless it is right in front of their face. Jan began to tell me about one dreadful day in February 2009. When faced with the massive crisis of the Black Saturday bushfires, she asked the question: 'what can I do to help?' This question sparked a reaction that turned into three years of intense hands-on ministry to the local community. While telling me this story, she quoted her pastor as having said, 'this is going to get messy'. The moment she said those words, something switched on in me.

'You have to tell that story,' I said to her.

Apart from the fact that it is a remarkable story of grace, courage, and sheer gut determination, it has so many lessons in it, learned by both Jan and her husband, John, during those three years. I believe some of those lessons are an encouragement to Christians the world over, no matter what sort of church you come from.

As we began the writing journey—me pushing them along—we found ourselves at the very date of the ninth anniversary of the Black Saturday bushfires. I realised I had opened a deep well of emotion in these people, as they began to recall and tell stories they had not thought about in a long time.

Soon Jan came to me and said she was worried this would make them sound like heroes—that compared to the people who had actually lost everything in the fires, their story was nothing. I understood what she was saying. Even though John and Jan saw the flames from close proximity, and in the months and years to follow, were immersed in the pain and grief of those trying to rebuild from the devastation, they weren't like the survivors. While that is true, what happened to them and people like them, was a significant event personally—working side-by-side, listening in shock to survivors who just had to talk, crying with people, lying awake at night trying to process the horror of what they had seen and heard. They did not lose family or possessions, yet this event rocked their world. As they tried to show Christ in the midst of utter destruction and knew that the old pat answers were of no value whatsoever, they also learned what it was to preach the Gospel without words.

'There have been many stories written after Black Saturday,' Jan said. 'I don't want this to be just a bushfire story.'

While we will read about the fire of February 7th 2009, we will also read about what these ordinary people learned, when hell was on their doorstep.

WARNING

Please read before continuing.

While editing this book, Jan questioned a couple of descriptions that had been included of some truly horrifying scenes. She was concerned that readers who may have suffered similar circumstances, may be traumatised by some of the descriptions.

'Is it necessary to include these graphic scenes?' she asked.

On the one hand, we would hate to open old wounds and cause people to regress to that awful time, but on the other, there is a phenomenon in our society that we might be able to speak to.

For some of us, we live in safe, comfortable Christian homes, and only see trauma and devastation on the nightly news. I am alarmed at how desensitised I have become to real horror. If I am disturbed, I can easily flick channels. Are you like this? This sort of emotional distance is easy to manage. Even if you find yourself in this easy state, it is not everyone's story.

PTSD (Post Traumatic Stress Disorder) is common in our society from a variety of causes. Retaining these few stories in this work may help people like me understand that this was not just another news story. This was not just about a working bee to furnish new houses. This was a truly devastating event—and it is good to remember that this kind of tragic devastation still occurs on a daily basis.

If you have suffered from PTSD for any reason, it is advised you skip these sections. If you have not suffered in this way, they are included to help you realise what real horror is about. When we come to that place of wanting to help, we will never truly know what folks have suffered when we haven't experienced it ourselves, but hopefully we can try to become more sensitive in our attempts.

Meredith Resce – author

Introduction

John Graham

When encouraged to write a book on our experiences working with bushfire survivors following Black Saturday, both Jan and I felt unqualified, as we ourselves were not survivors. When prompted to write what I felt, what I'd heard, what I'd seen, I questioned the value of it. I had been there and seen the flames and many other things, but I had only been an observer. What we experienced was from a distance, albeit a close distance.

Our involvement during the period following the most deadly bushfire in Australian history, proved to be a humbling experience as we walked alongside some of the people who survived the fires and who continued to live with the trauma of that time.

We are not heroes or experts. Simply put, we were in a place, confronted by a beast called trauma and grief, and all we did was put our hand to the plough. We were not the only ones. We were part of a team of people who, when the responsibility was thrust at us, took hold of it when others were not available at that moment.

You might say, 'right place, right time'. I would say, by God's grace, he filled us with his Spirit and guided us to each place at the right time. He stayed with us while we worked in a position no one was familiar with.

In writing this book, we hope to recount a number of stories and situations that occurred over the days, months and years following Black Saturday. We hope to share a little about what we learned then, and what we still have with us today, when it comes to being available to help in our community.

This monster fire front took 173 lives in less than 24 hours and the whole world saw and heard about it. The response was swift and came as aid was offered in many different forms. Now, ten years on, our challenge is to realise that there are thousands in our society who face crisis, pain and grief every day. Unlike when Black Saturday occurred, these people are isolated and often no one sees them.

What can we do? How can we reach out to help domestic violence survivors, families affected by alcohol or drug addiction, unemployed people struggling to make ends meet, or people living out on the streets?

Our hope is that this book will give insight into what some of us faced and how we responded. There was no choice but to respond, but we had no concept of the magnitude of what was before us. We took action moment by moment, hoping each step would somehow offer people hope beyond their circumstances.

As you read this, may you be blessed and come away with a new understanding of those around you who may be in need. Learning to look through Jesus' eyes will make the greatest impact for eternity.

Jan Graham

So why would we write a book like this?
What is it that would be of any value to the reader?

I have gone over these questions in my mind many times. We are not experts, we did not and do not have all the answers, but maybe that is it! It's easy as Christians to say out loud that 'God uses us to fulfil His purpose'; 'That we are to be the hands and feet of Jesus'; 'To love as Jesus loves'; and so on, but what happens to us when this is put to the test?

During the time of the Black Saturday bushfires, I have never felt more out of my depth. Having said that, there was never any doubt in my mind that this was where we had to be for that time. This gave me enough confidence to make the decisions that were needed. An overwhelming awareness of the prompting of the Holy Spirit was great comfort. Even in the noise and mayhem, it is absolutely true that we can hear that 'still, quiet voice' of God.

This is not meant to be an inspiring tale of how 'we answered the call'—I cringe at the cliché. Just as life doesn't always have a happy ending, neither does this story. We often stumble our way through ministry and pray that the Lord will fill in the spots we miss and make allowance for our mistakes. Although we are human and have all the shortcomings common to humankind, this is about God giving us what we need to get through. We are made in His image so we already have all the attributes of His personality.

Perhaps if we accept our weaknesses and embrace the strengths and authority we have in Christ, then the daunting will not be so terrifying. If we really believe that 'I can do all things, through Christ who strengthens me', then without pride, we can shake off the fear that can paralyse God's people—the church.

CHAPTER ONE
The Fury is Unleashed

Black Saturday, 7th February 2009

John

In Melbourne, a hot day usually means 30-36 degrees C (85F), but on this particular Saturday it was extremely hot. Some 46 degrees C (115F), and there was a huge wind building.

We had gathered together with other church leaders for a training day at a campsite near Upper Plenty, a region about an hour north of Melbourne, amongst the beautiful Australian bush. Other than the extreme weather, all was going along as planned. We were talking with friends over lunch when the owner of the campsite came into the dining room.

'There's a fire heading our way. Can everyone please stop eating and leave immediately.'

When he spoke these words, he used a calm tone. The request hardly seemed real. We did stop eating, but were not in any great hurry, still talking amongst ourselves and taking our time. When he spoke the second time his tone was firm—perhaps even desperate.

'Now!'

Suddenly, I realised this was serious and the need for us to move was urgent.

As we left the main building I noticed huge plumes of smoke in the distance. The general feeling seemed to be that the fire was still a long way off. We set about leaving, but at this stage, I presumed we would be safe. Almost everybody was still calm as they packed up and got ready to leave. In response to the campground owner's plea for help, two of our young men stayed back to help set up sprinklers around the centre.

It wasn't until the next day that I heard how close to tragedy we'd come. The flames had burned within five metres of the campsite, but the owner's relief was soon swallowed up by grief when he learned the fires had killed his brother on the adjacent property. My best mate had been the one to discover his body the next day.

As Jan and I drove towards home along the Whittlesea Road, we were mindful of our friends, Paul and Sue, who had a farm in that area. The smoke had continued to build and was frightening to see, especially considering that it was in the general vicinity. We decided to call in to see if Paul and Sue were okay. Little did I know that this decision to offer help foreshadowed something that would change the course of our lives forever.

As we pulled up to the house we saw Paul's daughter, Beck, up on the roof, clearing the gutters and blocking the downpipes with rags, ready to fill the gutters with water. Paul was rounding up his cattle to higher ground. We were well aware of the heat by now, not just that we were uncomfortable, but that with the wind now blowing at a ferocious rate, the conditions were catastrophic for bushfire. The activity on the farm was focused on preparing to defend the property. Paul hooked up his water tank to the tractor and then headed off to see if his older neighbour was all right.

Suddenly, in the midst of all this busyness, Sue received a call from their teenage son who was trapped in his uncle's house in Kinglake, which was being surrounded by bushfire. He was freaking out, crying and saying he didn't want to die, and then, suddenly, his mobile phone went dead.

Sue panicked and immediately contacted Paul to tell him about the phone call from their son. I can only imagine what they must have felt as parents. Paul had worked previously with the Melbourne Fire Brigade, so armed with his ex-MFB badge he got in his four-wheel-drive and drove straight towards the police barricades to break his way through to his brother's house where his son was trapped.

For the next 24 hours we lost contact with them and had no idea if they were alive or dead. Given the hell that had been unleashed in the Kinglake National Park and surrounding areas, we feared the worst.

With Paul gone, Jan and I did what we could to help get the property ready. I stood on their back lawn watering the surrounds of their house with a garden hose. I knew where the fire was—the smoke was an ever-present reminder—but when I turned in that direction I saw the most terrifying thing imaginable. Not just smoke now, I saw flames leaping about 50-100 metres above the treetops into the sky. I had never seen anything of this magnitude in my life. Even though the flames were probably still three or so kilometres away, I had a sinking feeling that this would be my last day on earth. I turned to Jan and told her to get in the car and drive into the Whittlesea township away from the fire that was heading our way. The sight of those flames made me feel so small and vulnerable against such an incredible force of nature.

Suddenly, the hot angry wind changed direction and the wave of flames quickly skipped across the top of the range from Wallan to Kinglake. At its peak, they estimate the fire was racing at up to 120 kilometres per hour. Once again, I saw things I'd never seen and never hope to see again. Trees about a kilometre ahead of the fire front looked as if they were self-combusting, igniting like match sticks, one after the other in succession.

I found myself transfixed, watching and hardly believing what was happening in the distance. The horror, the fear, the feeling of having no control, and no understanding of what was about to unfold.

This was the beginning of our journey into darkness in order to be bearers of light.

Black Saturday

Jan

John had just told me to leave him and go into the Whittlesea township. They had decided he would stay on the farm with Sue and Beck, while I packed my car with their important paperwork and documents. Even knowing that Sue and Paul's son could lose his life, I was on autopilot and didn't necessarily feel as if John was in any great danger. We had seen the wild winds push the fire back up the mountain towards Kinglake, and away from the farm. Of course, I didn't know what was about to unfold.

I headed down Wallan Road towards Whittlesea. The sky was such an unnatural colour, I could not have told you what time of day it was. In fact, I would not have described it as sky anymore—more just the atmosphere, which by now was a dark, orange/red-coloured thickness that had fallen over the area like a blanket. The visibility was poor and breathing had become difficult. Most of this was caused by the oppressive heat and the violent wind.

As I turned onto the main road, Plenty Road, it was starting to look like a war zone. The wind had caused havoc in the streets and people everywhere were out of their homes watching the smoke in the distance.

The first time I realised this was something bigger than anything we'd experienced before, was when I saw not one fire truck flying towards me, but a convoy of them—eight, nine, ten—all with lights flashing and sirens screaming. I saw a man using his shirt to try to flag one of the fire trucks down. His fence was on fire, and he was ill-equipped to deal with it in his shorts and bare feet. But not one of the trucks even slowed down. At that moment, I knew something terrible was happening on that mountain.

I left Whittlesea and drove home to Diamond Creek in a focused-daze, anxious to find out where my two kids were. Laura arrived soon after I got home, and I found out Ryan was with friends and was okay. Diamond Creek is one of the northern most suburbs of Melbourne, an area where the bush begins to merge with suburban housing. Although our home was not in any immediate danger, what I felt, and what I understand many felt on that day, was the awful sensation of not being safe.

ABC radio reporters were doing their best to filter reports through, but the chaos was obvious. Like any event, dreadful and alarming stories started emerging from who knows where. Some proved to be true, others were just an indication of the panic that was settling over this part of Melbourne.

By early evening, our house was full of people who had evacuated from their homes. For most, it was a precaution as no one knew which direction the threat may come from. The wind patterns kept changing and without being able to predict the direction of the fire, folks were feeling an overwhelming need to get away to safety. John didn't arrive back from Sue and Paul's until later that evening. He had kept in contact during the afternoon, but there was, in the back of my mind, the knowledge that the wind might change direction and push towards where he was. There was so much going on at this point that I was a bit robotic, just doing what needed to be done to get through the next five minutes. There was no time to stop and examine my feelings. Of course, there was some sense of relief when John finally did walk back through the door, into a house full of chaos.

None of us got much sleep that night. We kept the blinds open, ever watchful, just in case the fire should head our way. We had mattresses scattered across the floors, with children trying to keep cool and all of us constantly listening to radio news reports. We had many friends and acquaintances from our school and church community who lived in the Kinglake region, and no one knew what was really happening. We still hadn't heard anything from Paul about his son. There were a few stories that came through that we found difficult to believe. We heard of the kid's school friends standing on the roof of their home with their parents, fighting the flames. I thought there was no way this could be true, but in days to come, I found out that it had been the case. One of Ryan's friends had been on the roof, with his parents, using garden hoses to defend their home from the fire.

After the anxious and sleepless night, we emerged to face Sunday—a day that would only get worse as it went on. The news was on the television non-stop, and it was difficult not to watch, our horror increasing with every news report that filtered through. We watched in disbelief. Surely it could not get any worse. We were devastated when the first reports came in that up to a dozen people had died, with many homes and properties destroyed. The death toll was the most confronting, each hour more bodies were discovered and the list of missing was huge. Because this was our community, so many families we knew began to fill in the blanks about what happened. The face of the fire was so ferocious and loud—many survivors described it like the sound of a jet engine. The speed of the flames were such that no one could outrun it. So many stories.

Sue and Paul's Daughter, Beck Recounts Saturday and Sunday

It was around lunch time when the thick dark grey smoke started to come over the mountains. I was just leaving work in Whittlesea to go home for lunch and I saw it billowing in the sky. I ate lunch but didn't give much thought about what was to come. My brother's friend called and told us that Whittlesea was being evacuated. Obviously I wasn't going back to work. Tensions rose as Dad told me to help prepare to defend the farm, moving cows and making sure the gates were all open to allow them movement should the fire reach us. After having brought the furphy (portable water tank) up to the house, we hooked up the power generator and leads. If we lost power, then we would not have water pressure to fight the fire. I then went up on the roof to clear gutters and block downpipes. Then I hooked the hoses up to the gutters to fill them with water.

About this time, Dad left to help fight the fire on our elderly neighbour's property up the road. The flames had reached the ridge of the mountain, only a few kilometres away, and the wind was bringing it straight toward us. John and Jan were with us and helping in any way they could. Jan packed all our important documents and the dog in her car and left, while John stayed on to help. We watched, horrified, as massive fireballs jumped across the ridge. Houses on the hill were engulfed in fireballs in front of our eyes. Then suddenly the wind changed. What was a relief for us, turned into terror for the people in the densely forested area of Kinglake. The worst of it was that my brother was hanging out with a friend in that area. Mum rang my uncle who lived close to where Ben was, and asked him to go and pick up both the boys and bring them down the mountain. He rang back soon after to say that he had the boys but it was too late to head down the mountain. Access out was now cut, and they had no choice but to stay and fight the fires. What came after that was frightening.

We couldn't reach Dad who was still fighting the fire at our neighbours'. The phone kept ringing with various people asking ridiculous questions—well at that time, in our state of panic, the questions seemed ridiculous. People kept telling us to leave. At this point I took the phones (landline and mobiles) away from Mum and intercepted the calls. She had enough on her mind. My brother called a number of times from my uncle's house, which was now in the thick of the fire.

At one point, he was screaming through the phone, 'I don't want to die, I'm going to die Beck! Tell Mum goodbye... this is it!' Then he'd call back: 'I can't see anything! It's gone black! We've got no water pressure. I can't find Dylan. I'm going to die!'

I heard these phrases over and over again. These were hard words to hear from my brother and there was nothing I could do to help or calm him. My uncle's house had been surrounded, the sky went black. Ben said he could hear the screams of animals. He was on one side of the house with a garden hose and his friend on the other, with my uncle running between them. Somehow, they managed to save the house with two little hoses and hardly any water pressure.

When Dad finally got back from the neighbours', I told him that Ben was stuck up the mountain and that he kept saying he was going to die. Dad didn't wait a second, but hooked up the furphy, got Dylan's dad, Andrew, and headed up the mountain. Dad got through the police barricade by flashing a very old firefighter's badge and stretched the truth by saying they were only going a kilometre up the road, when in fact he was heading into the depths of danger.

So with Dad gone, Ben stranded and facing death and Mum frantic, I was left trying to play peace keeper. We lost contact with Ben after one last phone call. We had no contact with any of them and no way to know if they were dead or alive.

On the Saturday night, John stayed for a while but left around dinnertime. He had been a great support especially helping to keep Mum calm. By the time John left, my husband had returned home from working in the city, and my sister had come home. We sat on the side veranda of our house and cried as we watched the mountain and surroundings glow red. It was as if we were looking out onto a cityscape with all the lights. But we knew everything red and so eerie was not city light, but something so much more destructive. There was no sound but the crackle of the fire. We prayed for Ben and Dad to return safely, but Ben had said he was going to die and had said his goodbyes. We had no way of knowing if Dad had made it through or been caught up in the fire.

I clearly remember the Sunday night when they returned. Two seventeen year-old-boys, covered in black soot and smelling of smoke, were sobbing. They were exhausted and just fell in our arms and cried. We were so thankful to have our family back, but it was sobering to realise this was not the case for many people. I remember watching the news reports listing the names of those lost in the fires. As they rolled across the screen like credits of a movie, I kept seeing the names of people I knew. Name after name, after name.

Paul's Account

When I woke Saturday morning, I knew we were in for a hot northerly wind. While going about our normal Saturday farm tasks I noticed plumes of grey-white smoke in the north-west. Having fifteen years' experience as a professional firefighter in the Metropolitan Fire Brigade (MFB), I knew by the amount, colour and height of the smoke plumes that it was a very hot grass and bushfire. I kept an eye on it, watching the intensity of the smoke now rapidly increasing, and realised the fire had the potential to come in our direction. My daughter, Beck, helped me make some necessary adjustments at home and around the farm. I was well aware that we could face ember attack (embers being blown ahead of the fire front by the strong wind and setting bush alight). While looking back toward Mount Disappointment, an 800-metre mountain ridge covered in thick eucalyptus scrub, I could see my neighbour's farm just below the tree line and in the direct path of the oncoming fire. I rang to warn him of what was coming his way, as from their position, they possibly would not have seen what I could from about three kilometres further back.

His wife answered and told me her husband was on the tractor in the paddocks trying to cut some firebreaks along the boundary fences. She was upset that he was up there on his own. I told her I would come over straight away to help out. I hooked up the furphy on the back of my ute and headed off leaving John and Jan with my wife, Sue.

I was met by my neighbour's wife who was now extremely tense with her husband being up in the back paddocks without any communication. Though I wanted to head up there straight away to find him and help, she insisted I move their cattle into another paddock. The smoke was starting to intensify and I was getting anxious as I could now see the flames in the distance. The noise of it was like a jet engine. My mobile phone rang a couple of times, calls from concerned friends, and I had to yell into the phone as I was struggling to hear because of the roar of the fire. After seeing to the cattle, I headed up to the back of the property where I thought my neighbour might be.

I located him and after a heartfelt greeting, we decided to go back down to his shed and get a truck, which had a large water tank on it. Once we got back to the shed, we transferred to the truck and headed back up to where the thick bush of Mt Disappointment National Park met his farm boundary. We decided that while he drove along the boundary fence, I would get on the back of the truck with the fire hose and try to put out spot fires that were increasing on his side of the fence because of the ember attack. Within an hour it became obvious that the spot fires were getting beyond our ability to extinguish. We would chase and put one out, and then look back to where we'd just come from and it was burning again. The noise of the fire was terrifying. Even though we had wet rags wrapped over and around our face and mouth, the heat and smoke were starting to get to both of us. We were losing this battle, as fences were now burning as well as large portions of grass around us.

We had tried to persist by driving on the burnt areas up to the fast-moving grass fires. One of the main problems with this sort of grass fire is the amount of low ground smoke it creates, soon eliminating breathable air. We retreated back down the valley from the boundary of the farm. Suddenly, as we were heading away, one of my neighbour's sons came tearing through the smoke, driving a large earth-moving grader normally used for road making. He yelled instructions for us to get back to try and protect the house and immediate surrounds, while he continued cutting fire breaks with the grader.

By the time we got back to the house, fire was starting to burn around the house boundary on very short grass. We drove around and around the perimeter of the house just hosing the short burning grass. I knew from my time in the MFB, that once the fire has burnt the grass it would not be able to burn it twice, so the safest place most of the time is on the burnt sections. About half an hour later, I noticed another of my neighbour's sons and his mate had turned up and were using my ute and water tank to put out other small fires around the sheds and paddocks. After another hour of fighting the fire around the house, things seemed to be under some sort of control. The main fire had passed and was heading up the mountain towards Kinglake. I wanted to get home and see if everything was okay. As I drove the few kilometres to home I could see some houses were fully burnt and some half burnt, while others were just starting to burn in the distance.

As I drove up, I was thankful to see our house still intact, but that relief soon turned to anxiety once I pulled up. Sue told me that my son was up at Kinglake at his mate's house. Sue had already rung my brother who lived nearby to go and pick him up, which he had done. The wind had suddenly changed direction earlier and was now pushing the fire up the mountain range toward Kinglake. I rang my brother to let him know the fire was likely headed his way. My brother is usually an 'I'll be right' sort of person, so when he asked if I would come as it wasn't looking too good, I realised it must be serious. Without stopping to think too much about it, I decided I would head up onto the mountain to help my brother, who now had both my son, Ben, and his mate, Dylan, at his place.

Just as I was about to leave, Dylan's father, Andrew, drove up our driveway, concerned for the boys. I told him I was going to drive up to Kinglake and asked if he wanted to come. He said yes, so we prepared ourselves, filling the furphy with water and fuel, and making sure we had good thick clothing. After we'd driven through Whittlesea on the main road to Kinglake, we were stopped at a police roadblock. They were responsible for making sure no one entered the area, as it was now highly dangerous. That didn't stop me from trying to persuade them. The female police officer became irate—I imagine I was not the only one trying to convince her to let them through. She told me that if I didn't stop and turn back she was going to arrest me. I was frustrated and used a few colourful words to describe the situation. But I wasn't about to give up, so I told Andrew that I knew of another backblock route that would get us through. I drove about five kilometres to the back road, only to be stopped at another roadblock. This time I convinced the policeman that I was a fireman and showed him my MFB badge that I still kept in my wallet, even though I had left the MFB several years earlier. He consulted the Senior Sergeant who came over. After talking 'emergency services' jargon to him and giving him a detailed (and completely fabricated) explanation of what I planned to do, he allowed us through. The one and a half kilometres up the road, which I had told him, was actually nearly twenty kilometres, and I didn't realise I would be driving into the thick of danger.

Once he'd signalled to his colleagues on the roadblock to let us through, we drove slowly on. Just around the bend in the road I could see the main fire front had not long passed through the area, as everything was still burning on both sides of us. Now, my major concern was avoiding fallen power cables, as the crossbeams on power poles had burned through and cables had fallen over the road. I had no idea if the cables were still live or not. I calculated that if I stayed parallel to the overhead cables still hanging precariously, I would not be caught by surprise if they fell.

We got about five kilometres up the hill when we came across about eight fire trucks and crew parked to the side of the road. I was sure they would stop us, and worried that my previous exaggerated explanation (lies) that convinced the police sergeant, would probably not work with these guys. To my surprise, no one tried to stop us or wave us down.

A few kilometres further we turned onto the main road to Kinglake and saw more houses still burning, some houses that remained untouched, burned out vehicles on both sides of the road and people standing on the roadside—people standing out front of their destroyed houses, embracing each other. As we drove slowly past, some just stared at us with a haunted look in their eyes. It seemed that ours was the only vehicle on the road that wasn't burned and destroyed. I didn't stop to assist as it appeared there were enough able people to help each other, even though some of them were probably in shock. I was still focused on making our way through to my brother and son.

Driving in and out of heavy smoke and burning vegetation on both sides of us, we eventually got to the turnoff leading to my brother's place.

One of the local farmers waved us down and told us there was a large tree fallen and blocking the road to my brother's. He outlined an alternative route that would take us through the back of his farm, assuring us he thought it should be okay. I had listened to his convoluted instructions but as I drove off in the direction he'd pointed, I realised I hadn't remembered half of what he'd said, and as more colourful language surfaced, I just kept going. I remembered the part about going along the fence line, so I drove about 300 metres but by this time I couldn't see anything in the thick smoke. I was worried the ute would stall, as it seemed like there was hardly any oxygen for the engine to breath—something else I'd remembered from my training. The smoke was so dense it looked like night-time. Though Andrew had been with me the entire trip, we'd hardly exchanged a word, but now I spoke to him. I felt uncomfortable with our situation and told him so. He agreed that we should turn back straight away. By the time we got back to the farmer's house it was in flames. He was still there and indicated we should keep trying to get through. I wasn't going back down that fence line, so I told him I thought the other road was my best option. At least I knew the dirt road to my brother's place and I hoped we might be able to get through that way. One kilometre up the road, we found a thumping great gum tree blocking our path, still on fire, just as the farmer had told us.

Then, making a highly-trained fire-ground decision (not), I decided I needed to get through a fence on the left side of the road. I decided I would ram the farm fence by reversing the furphy into it. My logic was that the furphy would take most of the impact and damage. Just as I was getting the vehicle into position to ram the fence, the same farmer appeared out of the smoke on the passenger side of the ute. He said there was a gate about 50 metres back and that we could drive through and across paddocks, through a couple of gates on a course to my brother's place. This plan I was comfortable with as I knew where I was and what direction I needed to go.

We found the gate, crossed the two paddocks and found the driveway to my brother's place. Along the sides of the driveway, we saw all the haystacks around the tree line were still burning. I was anxious to see if the house—and my family—had survived the fire. I felt some wave of relief as we approached. The house still stood, but the paddocks were still smouldering. The fire had burned right up to his concrete verandas on all sides. My brother, his wife and the two boys greeted us with unrestrained emotion. They were so glad to see us and I felt exactly the same way. Without stopping, we immediately started driving around the property dousing as much smouldering stuff as we could, just trying to keep the smoke down. We then went further beyond his place to other unoccupied properties, dousing anything we thought would be a threat. We did this back and forth all through the night.

The next morning at sunrise we were sitting down having a break. Over breakfast we began to debrief. My brother told us what they had faced when the fire was roaring towards them. He had positioned the boys on opposite sides of the house, draped in wet blankets and each holding a garden hose. He was running between them trying to reassure them in the face of the terror that was upon them. I did not find out until later that my son had thought he was going to die. When I had spoken about this later, my brother acknowledged that it had been serious. He had been concerned mostly with the thick smoke and loss of oxygen, and had a last-minute escape plan ready to action if things got to the point where he thought the home was lost.

It was during this brief down time I realised there had been no phone contact with anyone from home. We had been so focused on the tasks at hand, watching to make sure smouldering stumps and other burning matter did not re-flare and cause more damage, that we had not noticed there was no phone communication. The phone towers had obviously gone down so no calls were coming in. The thing was, no one back home knew that we were safe, and given the news reports of many deaths and loss, our names had gone onto the MIA (missing in action) list. We did not know the extent of the worry the folks at home were under, but now that we had daylight again, we could see that the property was reasonably secure. Andrew borrowed one of my brother's cars and drove both Dylan and Ben back down the mountain late Sunday afternoon. Both boys needed to get home. They were physically and emotionally wrecked from what they had just been through, and, someone needed to let the others know we were still alive. The truth was, many people had not been so lucky.

I can't remember how I found out, but a roadblock was still set up and the police had rules to enforce. If we crossed over the roadblock we would not be allowed back up the mountain into the main fire zone. I felt I needed to stay up there and help my brother with what needed to be done in the face of the devastation, so we arranged for family members to meet us at the border and hand over jerry cans of fuel and whatever else we needed. It was like meeting at the Mexican border.

I stayed up on the mountain until Wednesday afternoon, and I saw many things that had resulted from the catastrophic fire, but I do not feel to share the details of what I saw. I have seen enough carnage to last me several lifetimes and prefer not to go there.

I found out later that my silent passenger, Andrew, had followed me into that battle, confident that my fifteen years of professional firefighting experience meant I knew exactly what I was doing. I've since told him I had never seen anything of that magnitude, and I had no clue either of what I was doing or what we would face.

CHAPTER TWO
The Shock Sinks In

Jan

Over the next several days, devastation turned to an overwhelming sense of loss. One hundred and seventy-three people had lost their lives, another 414 were injured, 2100 homes had been completely destroyed which left over 7500 people displaced—like refugees who could not return to their homes, as they were now homeless. It was estimated that 1.1 million acres of land had been burned and an estimated one million animals killed in the fire. Other statistics floated across the airwaves but by this time, it seemed impossible to process any more. I recall that there had been 5000 firefighters and that at least 78 towns had been impacted, five of them, including Kinglake and Marysville, completely destroyed. It is difficult to describe how the new statistics made us feel. We were numb with shock. At times, I even felt as if I was out of my body watching a bad movie. I'm not sure I really understood what those numbers represented.

The magnitude of this catastrophe was overwhelming. Victoria and, as we came to learn later, Australia had come to a standstill. We had not seen anything like this in our lifetime. But this wasn't just something we saw on the news. This was in our local area, and the smell of smoke and haze in the air was a constant reminder of how close we were to this tragic event.

I went to bed late Sunday and endured another sleepless night, lying awake trying to mentally and emotionally process the events triggered by this monster bushfire that was still burning. What could I do to help? In the face of such devastation, what could I possibly do? All I knew was that I had to at least try.

On Monday morning, I did not leave for work but called the office as soon as it was open. I was not worried that my boss might react badly to my not coming to work. I had been with the same company for over ten years and knew them to be compassionate and caring people. When I told him I would see if I could just help out today, and I would return to work in a day or two, I was not surprised by his response.

'If you feel you can help, it is important you stay,' he said. 'We are fine here.'

We were not the only ones who'd lain awake troubling over what could be done. Our good friend, Pete, contacted us early. He had the same sense of needing to do something to help. We decided to head into Diamond Creek. We had heard a relief centre had been set up there, and it seemed like the most logical place to go. We were so unprepared for what we found.

The streets were jammed with cars and people. There were emergency vehicles of every description parked near the local football oval, which had been turned into a makeshift camp for exhausted firefighters. Tents had been pitched and were now filled with food and water for those who had come in exhausted from the front and were waiting to return. It was like something from a movie set. This mess was not going to be cleared up in the next day or so. The fires were still burning and continued to do so for many weeks.

We made our way through the crowd to the community centre. It was full of people like us, wanting to help. As I looked around and studied the faces, I realised this was also a refuge for those who had fled the flames. I knew it was real but seeing people who literally only had the clothes they stood in, was sobering. If this was a movie, the camera would be scanning across the faces and capturing each expression, telling a story without words. It became obvious that many of them had no idea if their homes were still standing. Some had been separated from family and had no way of knowing who had survived. Thank God, Paul's son had returned to their farm by the Sunday night. Although the rooms were crammed with people, there was an unnatural silence—grief hung in the air, and everyone in the place kept their peace, respecting the pain and anguish that too many people were suffering.

The Answer Has to be 'Yes'

The Nillumbik Council and emergency services had come together and were doing a remarkable job under incredible stress and demanding conditions. I made my way to a man in a hi-viz jacket, who turned out to be the shift coordinator.

'How can I help?' I asked.

'Where are you from?' he asked in return.

'I belong to a church just down the road …'

Even as the words came out of my mouth, I had not thought any further than that. All I had in mind was what could I do today. I wasn't thinking big picture or long term. Who was, when hell was on the doorstep? But as the shift coordinator, he knew that what was going on in this location was not going to meet the demand. He needed to action something more and I, like the small boy who brought his two loaves and five fish to Jesus, said, 'I belong to the church down the road'.

I will never forget his next question as it sent me into a mild panic.

'How big is your church?'

What did he mean? How many people? How big is the church hall? Or was there something else behind the question that neither he nor I understood at the time?

'How big is your church?'

As time went on, it appeared this was not going to be just about property and people—this was going to be about heart capacity.

But at the time, I just answered as a normal person in this circumstance would.

'Well actually, it's fairly large, why?'

'What we really need is an overflow.' He answered without missing a beat. 'Is that something you could handle?'

Who did he think he was talking to? I was a church member, and we had small leadership responsibilities. But the question had been asked and he seemed desperate for an answer. He handed me his card.

'Please talk to whoever you need to and let me know as quickly as possible.'

Pete and I headed back to the church—our home church where we had attended for years—to have a conversation that I didn't even know how to start. On the drive there, I rang Pastor Paul Craig and told him we were coming to talk about what we could do to help the relief centre. I had no emotion. This was just doing what needed to be done. I had to do something. I had to be useful.

When we arrived back at the church, a few of the church staff met with us and Pastor Paul in his office. This was a thoughtful and prayerful time and though I didn't know exactly what he was thinking, I knew him well enough to know he understood what we were stepping into. I didn't believe he would say no, but there was a moment where I wondered what I would do if he did.

Pastor Paul asked us to pray together and seek God. In my mind there was never any doubt that we would act. We had to—we were the church. But in the back of my mind there was a temptation to just offer the help that I thought we could handle, which given the immensity of the need, wouldn't have amounted to much. Pastor Paul, however, understood that God was calling us to rely on His provision, His wisdom, His guidance and His ability to do more than we could ever understand.

Of the many stories, conversations, highs and terrible lows that I can recall from this time, this moment was one of those that is etched into my memory.

'It's going to get messy!'

I was unaware that Pastor Paul had already been to the evacuation centre on the Saturday night. He'd gone to offer help from the church however, because of the dire situation and scale of the operation, he came away feeling that they were more in the way at that time. He realised there would be an opportunity to help in the days to come. He explained to me later, that there was never a question whether we would help or not—it was always going to be yes. The question he was trying to answer was: what is the best way for us to assist? As it turned out, it did get incredibly messy, but it also became a gateway to our community in a way we could never have imagined.

The only reason for writing this book, given that there are many wonderful books and documentaries already produced about Black Saturday, is to tell the story about the things we have learned and the life-changing experiences that can happen when the church moves outside its walls. Back then, the answer had to be 'yes'. Today, if only we could see the depth of need that is hidden in the communities surrounding us, the answer still has to be 'yes'.

While Pastor Paul headed down to the relief centre, I made the call to the number on the card.

'Yes, we will be your overflow,' I heard myself say.

'Great!' he said. 'We will start sending people now.'

As simple as that. No paperwork, no three-day cooling off period, no time to think and prepare.

'The police will redirect the traffic to you.'

There was no turning back now. Within five minutes, a few cars appeared at the top of the long, curved driveway. The church building was situated at the back of a large property, and I stood at the bottom of the car park and watched a trickle of cars turn into a stream, to a river that seemingly had no end. The mild panic I had initially felt, was now full-blown fear. What have we done?

CHAPTER THREE
Emerging From the Chaos

John

Up until Black Saturday, I had been working as Victorian State Coordinator for Alpha—a course that helps people explore questions about the Christian faith. After Jan had connected the local relief centre in Diamond Creek to the Diamond Valley Baptist Church, our church building became an overflow for the donations stockpiling at the centre and an overflow for people needing to find a place of refuge.

Within hours, hundreds of people arrived at the church along with trucks, vans, utes and shipping containers to unload donated food, clothing and other goods for survivors.

Pastor Paul asked me if I would be willing to head up the relief effort on behalf of the church. I asked my boss for extended leave from work but within a few weeks, I knew I had to resign and join the church staff. This left Pastor Paul with the job to seek funding for my position through the Baptist Union of churches across Victoria.

It didn't take long for the media to arrive, wanting to film and interview survivors about the carnage that was taking place. Amongst the hundreds of people turning up to the church site were actual bushfire survivors. Having just seen the destruction of all they owned—homes and property—they had nowhere to go, so decided to come and help sort clothing and food alongside us.

It was surreal, watching so much activity, so much mess and so many people willing to serve. After a while I noticed that it was all just happening. No one had risen up to take that important role of directing everybody. Nobody saw this as an opportunity to gain status by taking control. We were all in this together. The barriers had come down. We had been thrown together with a common cause to help those in need.

Yes, it was messy and it was tiring, but for those who came to help, there was a strength that rose to the challenge—a strength we would all need to get through the unimaginable horror of the days and months that were to follow.

It wasn't just the people in the local community who rose to the challenge. Many more across the country and the world heard what had happened, and as a result opened their hearts and bank accounts, donating over $400 million to support the survivors.

An unbelievable amount of food, clothing and household items kept pouring into the temporary relief centre we'd set up at our church property. We soon filled our limit of eight shipping containers to store the goodwill donations. On top of that, local storage facilities offered free warehouse space and shop front storage across six other sites. These offers of space had originally been given through the local council but with limited resources, the council eventually asked me if I would take responsibility for this side of the operation.

Carpenters came to help build racks for storage within the containers. Cabinetmakers fitted out our church bus to make a purpose-built mobile relief centre to carry supplies up the mountain to the other relief centres. We made these trips three days a week over the coming months.

I still remember the first time we received passes from the council staff that allowed us to go through the police roadblocks. Pastor Paul drove our relief bus and I, along with several council staff, were jammed in amongst the emergency supplies. As we made our way up the mountain, the air was still thick with smoke. Once beyond the police barricades, we entered a world shrouded in ash and a sense of death. There was an unnatural silence. The sounds of birds and the wind in the trees, which one would usually take for granted, was conspicuous by its absence—just a vacuum where no sounds of life existed any more. The vegetation had been consumed, leaving only blackened stumps, and no animals had survived the firestorm.

In every direction it looked as if we had landed on the moon, or in a place completely obliterated by nuclear war. There was no colour, only the black of a tarmac road that had melted in sections, surrounded by grey ash as far as the eye could see. Miles upon miles of ash and smoke. Nothingness, emptiness, hopelessness. No fences, no means of distinguishing between properties. I can only describe what I saw as absolute devastation—a wasteland that resulted when two major bushfires met and consumed a third of Victorian bushland. As we drove slowly through and took in the awful scene, no one said a word. What could we say as we realised the immensity of the disaster and knew, at least in our minds, that this was a picture of death.

We reached the first relief centre at Arthurs Creek. It had been set up in a community hall that had survived the bushfires. A local man from Arthurs Creek volunteered to manage their relief centre. This was the first time I had met George (not his real name), but we became friends over the coming months as I returned in the supply bus. I showed him our inventory list and what we had on board and he selected what they needed.

Over the next few weeks and months, we established a regular path with our bus, travelling across Hurstbridge, Arthurs Creek, Strathewen, St Andrews, Whittlesea, Kinglake, Flowerdale and as far as Marysville to visit their relief centres.

WARNING – the following three paragraphs contain graphic description which may upset some readers.

These centres were operated by volunteers from the local community or by Salvation Army volunteers. An incident from one of these visits still haunts my memory, even nine years later. As we were unloading supplies from the bus at the Flowerdale relief centre, we were surprised when the Salvation Army officer in charge suddenly stopped in her tracks. She was staring into space and crying, and then began to say words that puzzled us.

'I kicked the log out of my way.'

Apparently, she had tripped over something in the main road of Flowerdale after the fires. I had no idea what she was talking about, yet I could see she was distraught. She kept saying repeatedly through her tears, 'I thought it was a log. I thought it was a log.'

Later on, I found out that what she had tripped over was a mother who had covered her baby with her body. Both had perished in the fire and before they had been identified, they looked like a log lying in the middle of the road.

Time after time we were confronted with horrific stories like this. Every day I met people who had been traumatised and were left without answers or hope. Though this was incredibly upsetting, I was determined to keep going and to try and find solutions where we could.

All we could do was listen to their stories and show practical love. This was not the time to try to answer questions that were too hard to answer—where was God during those fires? Why did so many people have to perish? Only God can answer those questions. We were sent to sit alongside those who were hurting and to offer practical help one day at a time, as they slowly began the process of trying to rebuild their lives. To sit, to listen, to help, to love and to pray silently.

CHAPTER FOUR
The Food and Clothing Bank

Jan

The following days were crazy. Cars, trucks, people. They just kept coming.

The goodwill of the community and the nation was overwhelming. Local people arrived with clothes and shoes from their own homes and the children came with their own toys to donate. Businesses sent whatever they had.

This was such an emotional week on every level but each time a car or truck arrived, I was humbled by the generosity and thoughtfulness of people. One delivery from a law firm in Sydney, had me confused at first as to what use the goods would be. They had given us a load of suits—all sizes and styles. It wasn't long before we understood that God had prepared the way for men and boys who had lost everything but the clothes on their back, to have something to wear to the funerals of family members. In hindsight, the gift was heartfelt, and it was sobering to see how much it was needed. We could not have orchestrated this.

Thank God for the truck load of tissues that arrived, for there were many, many tears.

Thank God for the lady who arrived with a boot-load of sanitary products. Evidence again of such deep insight into practical needs.

There were people who came to help from every walk of life, like many of us, needing to do something in the face of such an overwhelming crisis.

Early on, we had tried to create a system to receive all the goods but the donations flowed in so thick and so fast, it was difficult to keep up. Then I met June and Terry Warburton. June and Terry were local people who had offered to help down at the district council community centre and had then been redirected to us. June had experience in large retail management and Terry just seemed to know what to do next. They quickly established a flow and coordination of people.

There were so many wonderful people who came to help and at first, we didn't know who was who, or where they had come from. Over time, we learned that mixed among the volunteer workers were those who had escaped the mountain and left behind the ashes of everything they owned. They were numb and in the early days, most were unable to tell their stories. All they could do was what they were doing—unpacking boxes in silence, just needing to keep busy.

With all the coming and going of people and products, I was surprised when a friend handed me an envelope. She told me it was a voucher to buy shoes. I thanked her without thought and was ready to send it to be put with the other vouchers that had come in.

'No, no,' she said, 'this one is for you.'

She explained that a friend of hers had asked what they could do. She already had it on her heart to buy me a pair of runners and this person had bought the voucher. This was a nice thought, but if you knew me, you would understand that I am not a 'runners' type of girl. At first, I protested saying it was unnecessary, and even if I did decide I needed them, I could buy my own.

'Let them do this for you,' she said. 'You are going to need them!'

How right she was. I did go to the store and get fitted for some expensive runners, and my legs, feet and back were incredibly grateful. Some of our days were 15-16 hours long. This was just another example of people thinking of practical ways to support the relief effort. To this day I still have these shoes. Each time I see them it reminds me what it is like to walk in someone else's shoes.

The Nillumbik Council was a great support. They continually checked in with us to see what we needed from them—more volunteers, skip bins, packing materials and of course support staff for the survivors.

A few mornings after the crisis had begun, my alarm went off just as dawn broke. Everything ached and the tiredness was like nothing I had felt before. I made my way to the shower, then got dressed. I remember sitting on the end of the bed staring at the Nike shoes, trying to find the strength to keep moving when my phone pinged with a text message. It was from the same friend who had given me the voucher:

Just praying for you now and God has given me a scripture for you. Isaiah 61:1-6

> 'The Spirit of the Sovereign Lord is on me,
> because the Lord has anointed me
> to proclaim good news to the poor.
> He has sent me to bind up the brokenhearted,
> to proclaim freedom for the captives
> and release from darkness for the prisoners,
> to proclaim the year of the Lord's favour
> and the day of vengeance of our God,
> to comfort all who mourn,
> and provide for those who grieve in Zion—
> to bestow on them a crown of beauty
> instead of ashes,
> the oil of joy
> instead of mourning,
> and a garment of praise
> instead of a spirit of despair.
> They will be called oaks of righteousness,
> a planting of the Lord
> for the display of his splendour.' (NIV)

Here was a reminder of what we were doing. This is what I needed to help me get up and keep going. As I read this scripture I realised that this was more than a disaster response. This was the work the Lord had called us to do. I had been operating under my own steam and needed to take this moment to realign my focus and thoughts. We had been given the responsibility and privilege to be the feet and hands of Jesus to strangers, during a desperate time.

John

As the donations kept pouring into our church centre, we had to send these goods to separate locations and draft rosters of volunteers to manage these other sites for daily distribution to survivors.

A food bank was quickly established at an empty art gallery, opposite the miniature railway line in Eltham. More shipping containers were donated and delivered on site to be set up with shelving to store non-perishable foods. It looked like a mini supermarket with racks of nappies, canned food, cereals, biscuits, tea, coffee and bottled water—to name a few of the items survivors could come and collect without cost. Donations didn't just come from business owners. Ordinary people would buy extra while shopping, and deliver the goods to us to distribute.

As time wore on, we saw the need to set up tables and chairs with tea and coffee for survivors to be able to sit and talk when they came to collect goods. It became apparent they just needed to sit and download to people who would be willing to listen to their stories of survival. This was no pleasant afternoon chat on the veranda. These survivors were in the fresh stages of trauma and grief. We needed to mobilise people with a caring heart to be on roster—people who were good listeners. These survivors didn't need someone to talk at them and try to solve their problems (which was impossible anyway). They just needed to talk about the trauma and horror they had faced.

This is one thing I learned very quickly—be a good listener. Don't talk, just listen, encouraging them along the way.

So many stories filtered through our team of volunteers. So many tears and so much heartache. So many incredible stories of survival and even a few miracles.

I didn't realise at the time how important it is for volunteers to have an opportunity to debrief. What they heard and what they felt as they listened to so much tragedy and heartache, would become a burden difficult to bear. Unfortunately, there was no time for us to prepare for this role, and there was so much happening at the time, I did not have the time or resources for a daily debriefing. The result was a lot of lost sleep as I internalised the pain and grief of others.

Without the help of my prayer partners (Dave and Mark) who I met with most weeks for breakfast and prayer, I possibly would not have been here today. I heard some horrific stories which I will not recount here. I could not even tell Jan the things I was hearing, as I wanted to protect her from the trauma of it. While listening, I found most survivors did not apply filters to what they were saying. They just needed to get it out, and often did so in graphic detail of what they saw, smelt, heard, felt and their nightmares that followed. This left me with the burden of carrying their pain. If I had known then what I know now, I would have insisted that those volunteers who listened must seek counsel on a regular basis. I eventually knew I would need counselling, which I got, and ultimately, I studied for two years to be a Christian counsellor. If I were in the same position again, I would have trained counsellors as part of the wider team of helpers who could support the other listening volunteers.

Food and groceries were not the only items desperately needed. Families had lost everything and they needed clothes. We set up a separate clothing bank on the other side of town in Diamond Creek, in a building previously used as a vet clinic. Racks and racks of men's, women's and children's clothing were set up. Donations of toys and children's books were also made available. All survivors needed to have access to these donations was proof of their status by wearing a blue wristband or by being brought to these centres by their Department of Human Services (DHS) case manager.

With all the generosity and goodwill that had been extended, it was sad to learn that there were people claiming to be survivors, loading up their cars with free supplies, and later being caught trying to sell the goods to support addictions. Strangely, people from small communities have a way of identifying these people quickly as they know their neighbours and have a sense of who is legitimate and who is not. Even though there were plenty of supplies, we did not want to encourage wolves amongst the sheep as they can also be predatory when there are vulnerable people and children around.

It's ironic that as I write this, I'm making mental *notes-to-self* about what I should do if I find myself in this situation again—as if one can ever truly prepare for a natural disaster of this magnitude without warning. But as I said earlier, the tragedy, the pain and the loss still happens on a grand scale, only it is not in the open and usually in isolated instances.

Note to self - make sure to have a blend of men and women on your rosters at any given time of day or night to ensure the safety of survivors. When you have facility for change rooms or unlocked cars in the car park, the sad fact of life is there are those who will look for vulnerable situations to take advantage. Security can become an issue, even during a time when so many people are focused on doing good.

The Blue Forms
Jan

As the various government and aid agencies got organised, they put in place a system whereby those they considered fire-affected could be easily recognised. The folks who were walking in grief and loss were given either a blue form or a wristband, which they could show at relief centres to gain access to aid and supplies.

I found this very confronting. Though I have never been through times of war, I imagined what it must have been like to have no choice but to line up with ration coupons to get the bare essentials. This picture came to me when I saw these ordinary people—people like me—now labelled as 'affected', on top of all they were already experiencing through loss. They would arrive at the food bank with their forms. Most of them were people who had never had to rely on welfare, but their circumstances had dictated and they now had no control. At times it was embarrassing and demoralising for them. We tried hard to make this as comfortable as possible, but soon realised there was no easy way to receive aid, especially food.

This is another lesson for us today. Though the stereotype is often broadcast of 'dole bludgers' forever at the welfare office waiting on handouts, these are real people. Perhaps there are those who do not want to work, but how many others have been through loss—loss of job, loss of spouse, loss of health—and now find themselves, like these fire survivors, waiting in a line with a slip of paper? The new loss is upon them—loss of self-respect. I know how I felt for these folks at the relief centres. How much more today, when the loss is not evident, should we show respect to folks who are forced to receive handouts. This is a lesson in learning not to judge by the stereotypical, outward appearance.

John was spending a lot of time going up and down the mountain, and during these trips he became aware of many people who were in desperate need but did not want to ask for help. Those without homes had been scattered into emergency accommodation—some with family, some with strangers who had opened their homes. John is a listener, and he kept alert when news came via the grapevine of those who needed help yet would not ask. Whenever he got any information, he would seek out the full story and would quickly connect those in need to case managers.

When I learned of those who were not fire-affected but found ways to access the opportunity for free supplies, I felt incredible anger at the injustice. Thankfully there were not a lot, but I became fixated on weeding them out. While thousands were suffering, and many thousands of others had risen to give aid and donations, there were these few who lacked conscience and had no scruples in stealing aid supplies.

As a result of this righteous anger, I did not notice how my focus had shifted. Instead of my heart being fully engaged with the main job of being available to true fire survivors, my energy was being trained on finding out who these thieves were and how they should be dealt with. It took a while before I understood how much this internal vendetta was draining energy from me and, in the end, serving no purpose. I had to let it go. This was an internal struggle but the relief that came when I was able to readjust my thinking, was immense. I had to come to understand that I could not control people or their actions. Who knows why some people behave the way they do? Who knows what has driven them to feel the need to gather as much as they can. Perhaps they have other things going on in their minds and life.

CHAPTER FIVE
Gone From the Nightly News

Community Dinners
John

During the time I was distributing material aid up and down the Kinglake mountain, I saw many things that inspired me. One particular day, I went into the bakery and met a couple who were volunteering in Kinglake as caterers, preparing meals for large numbers of survivors on a weekly basis. One of them was a chef who, with his partner, helped to prep and serve the food. They were living in a van up the mountain.

Inspired by this initiative, I got a strong impression it was time for us to start hosting weekly community dinners at our church. I discussed this with Pastor Paul Craig who said to me, 'do you think survivors will come?' He was uncertain, given the long distance from our church to the various communities we were supporting, and also given that a high percentage of survivors had nothing to do with church.

I spoke to the catering couple I'd met in the bakery, and asked if they would be willing to come down the mountain once a week to cook at our church hall in Diamond Valley. They agreed and with the help of a few local volunteers, we were soon cooking for around 100 people every Monday evening.

It was amazing to see the response. We promoted the dinners through our regional network group and council staff, and encouraged anyone who was fire-affected to come for a free meal with an opportunity to meet other people with a similar story.

Before long, I invited people to provide some entertainment like Carter & Carter, an up-and-coming country music band, and other performers. This helped set a relaxed atmosphere after the meal for those who were willing to hang around.

Other Initiatives

Having seen just how debilitating PTSD (Post Traumatic Stress Disorder) can be and how many survivors were being affected by it, I decided to invite my counselling course lecturers to run some short courses to help address this issue. This initiative was designed to give survivors an opportunity to understand how the brain works and what happens when people face trauma. The course helped raise awareness and provide an avenue for people to meet and ask questions offline with the counsellors. It was apparent most would not travel and go to a clinic for this sort of help, especially if there was a fee associated with the visit. Once this program got underway, it helped to bridge a gap for some to get the help they needed from professionals.

As the first Christmas after Black Saturday rolled around, we realised the benefit of celebrating the extraordinary efforts of our volunteers. We threw a party, going all out with decorations, gifts for the volunteers and special performers invited to entertain our guests. These special people had been coming week after week and working tirelessly cleaning dishes or helping to set up and pack down. They had not wanted to be acknowledged as they wanted to serve behind the scenes. These are the unsung heroes, some of whom had nothing to do with our Sunday church congregation. They just came and served during the week.

Meredith

John's experience here highlights another important idea to remember. Sometimes we mistakenly think that only Christians are willing to serve in this humble way. This is far from the truth and as we continue to face great need in our society, we need to make sure that everyone who has a heart to serve, whether they are connected to a Sunday church congregation or not, be given the opportunity and resources to do what most recognise as the honest work of charity. Of course, with the rise in cases where people with dubious motives have used aid and church organisations to outwork criminal activity, we will always need to abide by the government Child Safe requirements to protect vulnerable people.

Back to the Real World
Jan

With John working in a more permanent role, it was time for me to return to my regular paid work. For a little over a month, we had been living in a very unnatural environment where every waking moment was filled with people in need, decisions to be made and problems to be solved. Now I had to readjust to the world outside of the Black Saturday recovery effort, and it wasn't easy. The rest of the country, although still very sympathetic, had moved on. Moving between the regular everyday world during the day, then stepping back into the aid environment at night was difficult to manage emotionally. The two worlds—so vastly different in terms of emotional response—were colliding. After a while, I felt as if I didn't fit in either world and I wanted to withdraw from both.

During those weeks working with the relief effort, I had met some amazing people and connected deeply with some. With the sudden confusion I found when the everyday world did not relate to the emergency-response world, I realised I needed to take a closer look at how I was coping emotionally. I cannot stress enough the importance of being self-aware when working in these types of environments. The old saying, 'give yourself a good talking to', is true. This isn't just as simple as telling yourself to suck it up and get on with it. That might actually be more damaging, leading to issues down the track. But it is okay to analyse your feelings and search out why you feel the way you do. When I took a close look, I realised I was upset that my usefulness had expired and that I needed to go back to the mundane daily functions. I was shocked at my thoughts, because I don't consider myself to be a selfish person. However, I realised that I was like many others, and had a need to be needed. This revelation didn't sit well with me. Not to be overly dramatic, but I did feel like I had abandoned ship.

When the Monday night dinners started, we thought only a few would come. We were surprised to see more and more people arrive. I cannot remember how many we would feed, but the food would always stretch. Again, volunteers would arrive to help prepare, serve and clean up—week after week. This was a vital point of connection for many. For me, it was a bit easier to leave after the clean-up and fall into bed but for John, it was a different story. After those community dinners, men would seek John out to talk until the early hours of the morning, standing in the cold car park in the middle of winter.

He was aware that the men were carrying terrible scars while still trying to be strong for their families. These long, into-the-night sessions birthed a whole new direction for John to cater for the men in the community.

Men's Getaways (VBRRA)
John

As part of my role, I was introduced to VBRRA (Victorian Bushfire Reconstruction and Recovery Authority). This rapid and unprecedented response by the government to the Black Saturday bushfires, had been set up just three days after the fire and was charged with the job to coordinate the rebuilding and recovery program. Some funding had been put aside for work aiming to help restore some of the survivors, particularly in the area of men's mental health. PTSD was understandably common amongst the folks who had been through this terrible tragedy and who had lost so much.

I met a number of times with different representatives from the community and VBRRA. Together we came up with a list of ideas we felt worth implementing to aid men struggling with PTSD. We planned for men to get away for day or weekend trips, hoping these trips would provide opportunities to normalise their life and build friendships back into their daily routine.

Over a period of time we arranged various group outings, taking along both volunteers and professional psychosocial support personnel. One of these outings we took about twenty survivors on a fishing weekend down to the Lakes District in Victoria. A few of my friends came along to support these men.

Early on the Saturday morning as we were getting set to leave, several survivors turned up drunk. The bus had not even arrived yet, and I wondered if we were in for some troubled times. Some of these guys were ex-bikers, rough blokes who had lost friends in the fires at Kinglake. One man, we'll call him Ted, kept to himself most of the time, just drinking and not speaking to anyone. As the weekend unfolded, the men took boats out to fish the lakes, two men per boat. Some decent-sized fish were brought in and we cooked them on the BBQ that night.

As we sat around in the pub after dinner, stories began to flow. I quickly realised that, as rough as these guys first appeared, they were broken men. Each of them had a story to tell, each of them had suffered their own form of hell on earth that weekend in February 2009.

WARNING—the following four paragraphs contain descriptions of a scene that some readers may find distressing.

On Sunday night, after our time of fishing and sharing, we got in the bus for the long trip home. I was sitting quietly when Ted, who hadn't said much all weekend, leaned across the aisle of the bus and cried into my face.

'What would you do?' he said.

'What do you mean?' I asked.

'If you crashed your car in dark smoke and saw a family trapped in a car, banging on the window, the car surrounded by fire, would you have driven off leaving them to perish?'

Suddenly I understood why he was trying to drink his way out of that nightmare. Night after night, month after month, seeing those desperate, pleading faces engulfed by flames and smoke as he smashed his way through the carnage, trying to get away from the fires. The trauma, the torment, the never-ending horror. I never saw Ted again. I do not know if he ever got the help he needed or even if he is still alive today.

What I do know is that because I was a part of that men's getaway, I was encouraged to put together my own program. I applied for government funding which was approved some months later. This time, I arranged a trip to Swan Hill. We took a bus full of men and met up with a church men's group from Swan Hill Church of Christ. We also arranged for a Christian psychologist to fly down from Queensland to run some workshops. He helped the men try to understand their thought processes, spoke on anger management and gave them tools to ease some of the stress they were facing.

On this trip we were based at a lovely golf resort on the Murray River. Here, men had the opportunity to either play golf, go fishing or just relax around the resort. Later we all gathered together over meals. It was here we were able to form friendships and attend some informal workshops either at night or straight after breakfast on the Saturday and Sunday mornings. Once again, I saw barriers come down between survivors and helpers, and bridges were built of mutual trust and respect. We just needed to be willing to sit and listen to their stories when they felt able and willing to share. I learned very quickly that just because I might be ready to listen, didn't mean survivors were ready to speak or share. I had to learn patience.

Not every tale of survival had a happy ending. For some, the loss was too hard to bear, and aid workers had to come to terms with this. Though trying everything to bring hope, some still slipped from their grip and were lost.

WARNING—the following five paragraphs contain descriptions of a scene that some readers may find distressing.

My Friend Bob
John

I had first met Bob (not his real name) on our Lakes fishing trip. He was part of a network group I had joined, and he had been sent from one of the government departments. His job was to distribute some of the $400 million in donated funds across the bushfire survivors. The network group was formed to meet weekly and report on what aid was being coordinated across the northern region of Melbourne. The group consisted of representatives from council, government, church, the bushfire community, and mental health organisations. Many friendships were formed as we worked together in a spirit of mutual trust and respect. No political power grabs emerged, rather cooperation amongst many hardworking people, both volunteer and paid staff, with a common goal to serve the hurting community on our doorstep.

Although Bob had a quirky sense of humour, I quickly discovered that he had a genuine heart for traumatised individuals and families. Many times, he got in trouble with his superiors as he overstepped boundaries by meeting survivors on their properties to personally listen to their plight.

As I worked alongside Bob, I got to know more about his personal life. I also discovered he had developed cancer. One day, I felt to visit him at home. I just wanted to see how he was and if I could help him. The last I had heard he was unwell and vomiting blood, so the next time I visited I took a pastor friend with a view to pray for him. It was an odd visit as Bob spent some time showing us his bank account and talking about his kids. It was almost as if he was settling his affairs. My pastor friend must have felt that also, as he asked Bob if he was planning to kill himself. It was a very direct question, and quite unsettling. I was relieved when Bob said no.

But that relief turned to grief when, the next morning, I received an email saying that Bob had committed suicide one hour after we left.

At this point, I hit the wall. I found myself asking what difference my Christian faith had made to Bob's life. Despite what my pastor friend had discerned, I had not been able to see what Bob was planning to do or stop it from happening. A good friend of mine had once told me, if ever you are going to lose it, go have a shower where you can cry, punch the wall, or whatever you need to do. When you return from the bathroom, your family will assume you got soap in your eyes. It didn't work. My family knew what had happened and sensed my anguish. My daughter came to my bedside later asking if I was okay.

I never lost faith in God, but I couldn't accept what happened. It was too close to home for me. It's difficult to know how much both the cancer and the trauma of working amongst bushfire survivors contributed to Bob's decision to take his own life. However, I can't help thinking that if he'd had more counselling or debriefing during his involvement with the relief efforts, there may have been a different outcome.

This was one of the events that contributed to my getting counselling and going on to study an advanced diploma in Christian counselling. I cannot stress enough how important it is to recognise our limits. We needed to set boundaries on how much time we spent in what we did, and we needed to know where and how to debrief each situation we encountered. From that time on, into the things we do today, I know we should aim to set up good accountability, including professional help—specialists who deal with this type of trauma on a daily basis. This work affected my sleep patterns to the degree that I still experience broken sleep and find it hard to switch off.

I have learned that I must let go of things and must rest in God in order to last the distance.

Temporary Village Fit Outs
John

We had been entrusted with a huge amount of material aid and, as I mentioned earlier, a team had outfitted our church bus for us to use as a mobile relief centre. As soon as it was operational, we made trips up the mountain, bringing loads of food, clothing, groceries and other necessary items to survivors.

Over the next three months of visiting the relief centres up in the mountains, we got to know the staff who operated in each region. We also got to know who the gatekeepers were. These were the folks who took it upon themselves to keep sightseers and any potential mischief-makers away from the locals who were doing their best to recover. In the regions of Kinglake, Flowerdale and Marysville, temporary villages were being established for some of the bushfire survivors, given most houses had been destroyed.

One day we took our bus to Flowerdale. This little town had lost more than three-quarters of their homes and was one of the places where a temporary village had been set up. Soon after we got there, I walked across the football field towards the temporary village manager who was talking to two men in suits. The manager was obviously furious, swearing and waving his hands around, telling them to f... off, just as I walked towards them. This was somewhat unnerving, but I pressed on, while the two suited men went straight past me, red-faced.

'Who are you?' the manager bellowed, obviously set to get rid of the next lot of annoying intruders.

'I'm John,' I said, trying to maintain some confidence in the face of aggression. 'I'm from the Baptist church down the mountain, and we've come with a bus load of supplies. How can I help?'

He put his arm around my shoulder and shouted out after the two retreating men in suits: 'This is what I need! Not idiots trying to tell me what to do!' Apparently they were from a government department and this local gatekeeper hadn't taken kindly to their directives about what they thought the locals should do.

'Come with me,' he said. He took my list of supplies to look over and then started to show me around all the dongas (miners' huts). The huts had been delivered, but now the locals needed help to fit them out, and here we were to help.

After having reviewed what would be needed, I went back and organised a team of volunteers. We returned with the team for a day of hard work. We came loaded up with prepacked goods to fit out each donga—linen, crockery, cutlery, toaster, kettle, pillows, etc—and we worked to clean each unit, making it fit for families to be able to move straight in.

On another occasion I was asked to go up to Marysville and look through their temporary village and recommend what was needed to fit out the dongas that had been donated to them as temporary accommodation. On the day I arranged to go I was delayed by unforeseen circumstances and being late, ended up arriving at the same time as a fleet of cars.

My tour guide was the government-appointed manager on site to oversee the setup of the facility up until handover. He looked at me and the large group of people who'd arrived at the same time, and I could tell he was concerned. I felt slightly awkward given that I was late, but he apparently decided to push on regardless.

'Okay let's go,' he said to all of us, and we set off together, walking around the temporary village. The group included a couple with their children, and the others from the entourage were fussing over this family, offering bottled water and muffins. The family seemed relaxed amidst this special attention. I struck up a conversation with the father who asked me who I was and what I was doing there?

'I'm John from the Baptist church down the mountain,' I replied, 'and we're here to scout out what's needed by way of material aid and manpower so that I can organise a team to come back and fit out the dongas. This needs to be done before survivors can move in.'

'Keep up the good work,' he said. His wife seemed complimentary of our team also.

'Where are you from?' I asked.

He explained that he and his family had just returned from a holiday in Hong Kong, and they had just called in to see how things were progressing at Marysville.

At that moment someone spoke to him, and it was his cue to move. All the folks returned to their cars and the entourage drove off.

The manager of the Marysville temporary village looked at me in disbelief.

'Do you have any idea who you were speaking to?'

I didn't, but the comment about dropping by on the way home from Hong Kong probably should have given me a clue.

'That was Andrew Forest and his wife and children,' he explained. 'They have borrowed Packers' chopper, which landed in a back paddock.'

Andrew Forest, is a mining magnate and one of the richest men in Australia. I had not seen the chopper. They had landed in the back paddock to avoid any media coverage. These were all his dongas. He had donated them and paid for their transport across the Nullarbor from his mines, to the front line of the bushfire affected areas. After having chatted with him for a short time, I felt like I knew him at a personal level. Andrew Forest and his family seem down-to-earth people, and he had a generous spirit. We are all greatly valued and loved by God no matter how rich or famous, but it was a privilege to meet them. This meeting helped me realise that this tragedy had stirred the hearts of people from all walks of life.

Several months later I spoke with the manager in charge of the temporary village at Kinglake. We arranged a time for me to come back with a team of youth volunteers, ready to clean and fit out each donga across their village. It was an amazing experience and rare opportunity for youth to engage with survivors, and be able to show practical love and support at a local level.

As Time Moves On

Ten months had passed since the fire and we were approaching the first Christmas since Black Saturday. I suggested to our church that we take the music worship team up to the Kinglake village to bring our Christmas carols to them. I was disappointed when it was decided, after some discussion, that it would put too much strain on the team at a busy time of year. They did not believe they would be able to conduct two carol service specials with all the set up and gear required—one up the mountain and one back at home base. I had to come to grips with the fact that not everybody saw the work up on the mountain the way I saw it. My passion was not their passion. At this point I realised that some saw our church pouring out so much resource and effort into this bushfire relief process, and it had already been ten months of giving. Other ministries were struggling to maintain with limited time, people and money.

I was grateful for the Baptist Union who helped come up with funds for my position for the first three to six months. They were able to see that people were desperately required on the ground—necessary to find the greatest need and provide accurate reports on how best to respond.

Part of my position was to release aid by recommending how $188,000 worth of relief funds was to be distributed. Over a period of months, as I heard about particular families and individuals who were struggling with the loss of home, possessions and in some cases the loss of family members, I was able to assess the need and release funds.

The frustration came from not having enough funds or human resources to respond to every situation that became apparent. That frustration continues every day for people who are passionate about meeting the needs of a broken and hurting community—there are never enough funds and never enough people on the ground who are as eager to give as the needs that exist.

My advice to anyone wanting to reach out to community needs would be to make a clear call to action. State plainly what is required at that time. Gather those who have a similar passion and establish realistic expectations of what may be achieved. It is always better to promise less and then have the opportunity to over-perform. You may arrange to mow the lawns of someone who is sick and incapacitated, and end up bringing a team of people who also slash along the fence line, clean all the windows, bring a cooked meal and a hamper of goods to restock their pantry.

The response from recipients is nearly always full of gratitude. There are plenty of times when you want to do more but are unable, due to lack of personnel or the physical fitness of the available volunteers. Capacity will always play a huge role in your output. What you say you will do is dependent on what resources you have access to at that time.

I found out where my weaknesses lay when I quickly got frustrated by things out of my control (mostly people). I developed a 'can do' attitude by not letting things stop me. I would rather refer to these challenges as speed humps that are more designed to slow me down.

There is always another way to get something done. You just need the patience to figure out a better way around the problems you will face in life.

Community Guardians
John

The first day I met Fred (not his real name) at one of the relief centres, I felt as if I was being interrogated.

'Who are you? Where do you live? What are you doing here?'

He wasn't there to welcome me in his loud, gruff manner, and though he was the first person I saw, I'm not sure he was there as a public relations officer, between his spitting and smoking and straight-to-the-point grilling.

I soon realised that Fred was the self-appointed gatekeeper for this battered community. He was rough and intimidating, and I'm not sure everyone appreciated his police-style protection—making sure no stickybeaks, looters or other unwanted persons intruded into the recovering community. No one was going to come in and get material aid from Fred's relief centre unless they were genuine.

Over time, I saw past Fred's rough exterior and realised he had a soft heart. He had lived locally all his life and had a daughter who was dying. With the help of my two mates, I decided to work on Fred's house. He needed to finish off some floor tiling for his daughter who had moved back into the family home. Fred and his wife were her full-time carers.

Fred had a family business that connected him with most of the people around his community. Through these connections Fred introduced me to many people who needed help—people who had fallen through the cracks of the system and others who wouldn't come and ask for help after Black Saturday.

Fred and I built a mutual respect and friendship, even though he regularly told me he was a heathen. Fred would take great pleasure jumping on our bus and travelling with us up and down the mountain, delivering material aid to the relief centres. Whenever the bus would stop, he would be the first to jump off and announce to the people, 'I'm the only heathen on the bus, and this is John the Baptist!'

This is how I became known as John the Baptist, up and down the mountain, even when being introduced at community meetings. To me it was a term of endearment and respect, and I didn't see it as a put-down. Interestingly, my Christian mother says she named me after John the Baptist, who was mentioned in the Bible as a 'voice in the wilderness' and a forerunner to Jesus.

Finally, Fred's daughter was able to have a life-saving operation. Fred called me and asked if Jan and I would meet with the family at the hospital. Of course we went, and prayed for them during the eleven-hour operation. It proved to be a success—praise God.

When I think about it, I am amazed at the opportunities I've had to connect with people on a personal level during those three years working with bushfire survivors. From one of the richest men in Australia, Andrew Forest; both prime ministers, Kevin Rudd and Tony Abbott; council workers, mayors, emergency-service officials, and Fred.

At the end of the day we all have a heartbeat and capacity to reach and impact other people. It is what we do with our life that counts, not just what we can get out of life.

Meredith

I want to talk about the type of frustrations John and Jan encountered because it is real across the NGO and charity world. We have to come to grips with the fact that what motivates folks like John and Jan to continue being available, even sometimes to their own personal detriment, may not be the same for other people. There is never a shortage of needs to be met, but not everyone sees those needy situations through the same lens. How I prioritise my time comes from my perspective and what motivates me. I need to understand that others may see the same situation differently, and have different priorities as to how they may or may not respond.

When Black Saturday was roaring in our backyard, emotions were high, and nearly everyone felt the need to offer help in some form or other. But when the flames are no longer obvious, life for the unaffected goes back to normal. The human pain is no longer being telecast to the world, and people forget that hurt and broken individuals are still there. On one hand, I don't want to lay a guilt trip on those who are happily working and living a comfortable family life, but I do want to raise the discussion, because sometimes folks don't extend themselves because they are unaware. It is not so much a case of they don't care, more a case of they don't see. When we could see the devastation of Black Saturday every day in the news media, people responded.

Many charity organisations have promotional drives—frequently. Compassion fatigue has settled upon us as a western society. One of the most alarming things about compassion fatigue is not only that it is now a coined term with a dictionary definition, but that it is real.

Compassion fatigue—an indifference to charitable works on behalf of suffering people, experienced as a result of the number of appeals.[1]

You've surely felt it. Once you give to an organisation, you will be constantly bombarded by mail and emails alerting you to the desperate need. The temptation is to unsubscribe. I want to look at this in more depth later in the book. The old WWJD adage—What Would Jesus Do—must inform this situation to some degree.

We are being made aware. But it is a little like visiting certain countries where begging is a normal part of society. As a westerner, if you give to one beggar, then you will have a multitude of beggars milling around you, beseeching you to also give to them. What a conundrum. Do you care? Of course you do. Are you an endless supply? Well therein lays the difficulty with any care work that you might either give to or put your hand to. This bears further discussion.

Part of the purpose of this book is to say: we know you care, let us help you to see where the need is and how you might be able to help. But as John said, you will need to be realistic about what you can give, how you can give and when you can give. Under promise, over deliver. But don't become indifferent.

---

1. Google online dictionary

CHAPTER SIX
I Never Saw This Coming

Jan

We had been focused on the relief effort for eleven months. Setting up and running the food and clothing bank, organising the community dinners, being on hand to listen to story after story, and cry.

WARNING—the following story (3 pages) contain descriptions of a scene that some readers may find distressing.

Then one day in early January 2010, I received a call from one of my closest friends. We had been friends for over twenty years and usually met for coffee at least three or four times a week—sometimes a long chat, sometimes a quick catch-up on our way to somewhere else. On this particular day a text came from her.

Can you meet me?

I replied straightaway, and we arranged to meet at one of our usual places. As I walked towards her I could see the tears streaming down her face.

'I think I need some help,' she said, without preamble.

I had been aware that she was struggling with a few different life challenges but had no idea of the depth of despair she was feeling. I suggested we move our catch-up to somewhere we could talk without strangers looking on, so we went back home and sat on the deck. For many hours, she opened a vault of deep thoughts and despair. I remember watching her face, thinking, how did I miss this? How could I be so focused on the urgent and obvious ministry with bushfire survivors, and yet not recognise the signs of a cry for help from someone so close to me?

My friend's emotional condition deteriorated, even with great support from family and friends, and several medical professionals. Each story of those who suffer with anxiety and depression is unique. The treatments and processes can be similar, but each person's story, their individual strengths and weaknesses through troubled times, cannot be compared.

After great care and counsel, my friend voluntarily admitted herself to hospital. Then it became necessary for her own safety to have a more permanent stay in an adult acute psychiatric unit. My visits were spent with her agonising over how she had gotten to this position. She was fully aware of her circumstances, she understood the condition of her mind and it was her desire to be well. She tried as best she could to cooperate with the programs, but all the time she was confused as to how this had happened. One of her main concerns was how this was affecting her family. She did not want her children's lives impacted by her emotional state.

A day's leave was granted and on a rare moment when she was alone, my friend took her own life.

This still feels like a horror story that we were watching, yet we were part of it and had no control over what was happening. On one hand it was so real, but on the other, it was like living in a parallel world. Even now, after several years, I find myself wondering if it really happened and perhaps it was just a very bad dream.

The personal loss I felt kept me paralysed for a long time. It felt like a dark vortex that kept spiralling and I was being sucked deeper into the blackness. This could not have happened, but it did.

I questioned everything I knew about ministry and care. Does anyone get well? Of course, we know that people do recover and healing does come, but when the loss is personal it robs you of the ability to think straight, let alone have a positive thought.

I remember thinking: *this is what it feels like*. Suddenly I understood the scars a tragedy can bring to your soul. The physical pain in your chest and body, and the overwhelming feeling that this would never be okay.

Prior to my friend's passing, I had sat with bushfire survivors who had experienced this feeling, but I'd had absolutely no idea what they were going through. On reflection, I was grateful that usually I'd said very little to survivors as they'd poured out their grief. I may have had something wise or comforting to say, but now I understood, there are no words that are of any comfort when such grief has entered your life.

The day my friend died, my dear friend Beth arrived. She didn't say a word. She held my hand and we just cried for a very long time. My friendship with her has always been strong, but these life journeys can create a depth of relationship that lasts a lifetime. I am truly blessed to have wonderful friends and family in my life who at any time, and especially on this day, just come to share the grief.

It doesn't seem right to only have a paragraph or two to describe this time—She was such a special friend—but the purpose of disclosing this part of my life is to share with you how it was that I started to understand. How I began to understand the complete numbness that quickly deteriorates into apathy. Well-meaning people may offer thoughts like 'time heals'. I may have offered these words myself, but now I know that it doesn't. Time just gives you space to create a different brain pathway without this person in your life.

During my time of deep grief, someone shared the following word picture with me. They encouraged me to imagine that I had walked into a very deep lake and I was at the deepest part where the water was way over my head, and I had no access to the air supply cut off by so much water. They encouraged me to see myself, and if I could keep moving, even if I could only take small steps, and even if it was very slow, the water would eventually become shallower. I found this picture helped me navigate through some of the very dark, confusing and even, at times, violent thoughts.

Life is unpredictable. We don't know the script. I believe we should make plans and cherish those close to us. Pray for strength on the tough days and rejoice in the blessings. I have understood that the only things I can be responsible for are my thoughts and my choices along the way. I know myself better now—my weaknesses and strengths. Above all I know that Jesus is not just a fictitious character who I can pull out when needed. As the psalmist wrote, '[He is my] very present help in times of trouble'. Psalm 46:1 (KJV)

CHAPTER SEVEN
Rising From The Ashes

John

Months after the Black Saturday fires, I was still working alongside survivors and hearing many deep and heart-rending stories. God began to speak to me about becoming the voice for the unheard—about offering hope to many others who had survived. To do this, God inspired me with the idea to make a documentary film, and to call it *Rising From The Ashes*.

    I had never done anything like this before, so I went to a friend who works in film production. I shared my vision with him and told him how I might be able to gather several stories from a range of survivors. Young and old, single and married, Christians and people with no faith affiliation—people from across several of the hardest hit areas. I pitched the idea that I believed we could get survivors to tell not only their stories of loss and devastation, but also how they have journeyed on, picking up the pieces and getting on with life—step by step and day by day. I told my producer friend that I could see this film offering hope to others who had endured similar trauma.

    My friend reflected on everything I had put to him, and said it was an incredible idea. However, he also said for me to come back to him when I had $50,000 to fund a film crew and editing team, and to develop promotional material to market the film.

On hearing this, I was deflated as coming up with $50,000 sounded impossible. But in just three months I had found ten sponsors who were willing to put capital into the project with no expectation of return on their investment.

With the means to go ahead, I was then faced with the challenge to find eight people who trusted me enough to be willing to be part of *Rising From The Ashes*. They needed to be people who understood that as they poured their heart out in front of the camera, they were making their story available to thousands of people. They were making themselves vulnerable. I approached eight fire-affected survivors who agreed to be in the film.

Over the next six months, we filmed 200 hours of footage, which was edited down to just 56 minutes. We made it a suitable time length for television presentation, allowing for commercials, as a documentary. As we'd hoped, the survivors who consented to be involved were able to tell their stories of hope in the midst of trauma.

As we finished the editing, we approached a number of television networks in the hope that one of them would be interested in airing the production. This presented us with an ethical challenge, as every channel we approached wanted direct access to those survivors who featured in our documentary. They wanted to put their own spin on the story, which would not only detract from the original concept, but be a breach of trust between the survivors and myself. I had given my word that each person would be able to preview the film and have input into the editing. They needed to see how it would be presented and have the confidence that their stories would be treated with respect and care.

Given the pressure the various networks put on us to expose our contributors, we decided not to sell the rights to any of the networks. In the end, we decided to keep it simple. We planned to premiere the documentary at Diamond Valley Baptist Church fifteen months after Black Saturday.

In May 2010, over 600 people came to the premiere of *Rising From The Ashes*. At the conclusion of the film, the survivors who had shared their stories stood on stage to the thunderous applause of the audience. I had arranged for 500 copies of the DVD to be given away as gifts to people who had experienced similar trauma. I hoped that it would help to raise awareness of PTSD and the ongoing effects where people need support. Some of the people who attended this premiere included those who had been coming to the community dinners. During the fifteen months since the disaster, these people had bonded and formed friendships. We saw the community spirit that had literally risen out of the ashes. When they received a copy of the DVD, there was an overwhelming response.

To give away love without any expectation of monetary return, sometimes comes back ten, fifty, or even one hundred times greater than you would ever expect. The friendships that formed were the return on this investment. Trust and respect had been earned over this time. Many survivors and volunteers working hand in hand throughout the community—Kinglake, Strathewen, St Andrews, Flowerdale, Hurstbridge and even the Nillumbik Council—developed a bond of friendship that one could never buy.

It was amazing to see God at work when personal agendas were put aside. In the instance following Black Saturday, and in any situation you may see today, when the primary focus becomes the welfare of others, the rewards are immeasurable.

You can view the documentary *Rising From The Ashes* on You Tube.
https://www.youtube.com/watch?v=FOYR_SwZ3d4

CHAPTER EIGHT
The Local Community Rises To The Challenge

John

In 2010 the assistant principal from one of the local high schools approached our youth pastor asking if we could involve their Year 9 students in the relief effort. They were offering us 200 young people to help bushfire survivors. After a number of meetings and discussions with senior teachers and community leaders, I helped to formulate a plan, deciding which properties these mostly fifteen-year-olds could work on.

This proved to be a massive project with regard to risk assessments for each and every property. Parent consent forms, bus schedules, remote mobile phone access, teacher rosters, Working With Children Checks, and all of the government compliance administration that needed to be done. Hundreds of students working on many different properties over many months was never going to slide by the Child Safe authorities without them demanding some intense scrutiny and reporting on every level.

Just in terms of the required risk assessment forms, that need to be filled in before any student goes off campus, was a logistical nightmare.

We had to come up with an assessment about how we would control and keep safe up to twenty kids at a time—kids who would be running around snake-infested properties with slippery-surround dams, wild dogs and traumatised survivors who did not handle too much noise or pressure very well.

In the natural you wouldn't touch this with a barge pole. But with a lot of prayer and wisdom, we were able to work with the teachers and the community to bring together an amazing experience for all concerned. Most of these students were typical cheeky, rowdy fifteen-year-olds, with a few who were withdrawn and who kept to themselves. However, we knew the plan was working when they begged us, at the end of a long, hard, tiring day's work, to go back to the same property for a BBQ. They had formed a bond with the family who had been living in a tin shed since the fires. This family now wanted to put on a BBQ for the kids who had helped clear their yard and stack firewood; who had helped rebuild a shed and sort rubbish into piles. This was one example of the student work parties. These students were looking outside of themselves and found a heart for those less fortunate. They truly discovered the meaning of, 'it is better to give than receive'. Something greater than themselves was being imparted through the spirit of generosity. This was a life-changing experience for those students.

Sadly, not all stories end well. Life is about choices. Unfortunately, life choices can sometimes take people to very dark places leading to anxiety, depression and ultimately a place with no hope. Even though a new house was eventually built on that property, I found myself at that friend's funeral after he committed suicide seven years later.

It was because of events like this that I was originally prompted to produce, *Rising From The Ashes*. Standing at the funeral of a man who had lost all hope, I was desperate to find a way to try to point others, in the same situation, toward hope.

I lost count how many properties the Year 9 students worked on. They helped young and old, single and married survivors. It was a truly amazing experience that none of us will forget. Yes, it was hard work and yes, there were many difficulties to address. Would I do it all again? Yes, I would.

I learned to avoid forming my opinions based just on what I could see or what I thought I understood. The natural mind rarely has the foresight to see the potential fruit in each person—especially boisterous, noisy fifteen-year-olds. It sometimes takes the leading of the Holy Spirit to look beyond what we naturally see and have faith in what is yet unseen.

Diamond Creek Men's Shed
John

During 2011, a group of men in the Diamond Creek area called a public forum to seek expressions of interest to form the Diamond Creek Men's Shed as an initiative to address men's mental health. The main problem was they did not have a venue for men to meet even though there was great interest.

I had been invited to attend and I spoke at that meeting. I came away with the charge to investigate the logistics of what was needed by way of a venue, and to explore the possibility that it could be housed at our church. We had a large garage on site, and a shipping container that could store their equipment.

By the end of 2011, I had liaised with our church leadership and put together a proposal that was acceptable to the church. We were able to draw up a formal memorandum of understanding between the newly formed Diamond Creek Men's Shed and Diamond Valley Baptist Church.

This group quickly outgrew the church's garage and shed area, which was a good problem to have. Even though a great partnership had grown between the church and the Men's Shed group, it soon became apparent that they needed to move to a larger facility by the middle of the following year.

They relocated to a scout hall in Diamond Creek and have since received funding from the Bendigo Bank and the State Government.

The latest figures say they have grown to over 90 members, which is fantastic.

One of the members recently wrote:

'This *shed* is about *men's* health and giving support to the community. What most people don't know is that this *shed* assists and supports its own members when they are unwell or doing it tough. I have been a recipient of this support and it h*as* been enormously beneficial to me through a difficult time.'

The Men's Shed Association is one avenue that helps men with PTSD. This is especially evident post Black Saturday, where being a member of the Men's Shed has helped reconnect men to support. It has given them a community where they have been able to share their experience and receive practical support and ongoing friendship.

More and more we are finding men who have lost their identity and self-worth, particularly post retirement. Anxiety and depression can overwhelm in many cases, and these men need mental health support. There is a high demand for mental health professionals.

Counselling and training can play a huge part in this growing area of need.

CHAPTER NINE
Who is My Neighbour?

Meredith

When hell is on the doorstep, I doubt many would draw back from helping to meet the needs. The story that John and Jan have shared in this book shows just how people of all situations, with or without faith, are willing to go to great trouble to be part of an aid effort. This story reflects, with credit, the heart of many in the community affected by the Black Saturday bushfires—selfless, willing, tireless, generous, persistent, kind and caring. Many people put their hand up to help in some way or another.

What I said earlier, that the fire is still burning, is what I want to focus on in this chapter. We live in a world where we can, if we choose, distract and distance ourselves from trial and brokenness. Sometimes trouble comes and finds us where we live, as in the case of Jan's friend. In our middle-class western social structure, however, we often have the means to furnish a comfortable environment. I like comfort, I won't pretend I don't. If we don't want to be aware of the trouble in the world around us, we flick channels and don't watch the news. We recycle the charity letters pleading for assistance, we make fun of social justice warriors who make it their business to wave placards and guilt us into taking action. That compassion fatigue is real, and sometimes the needs seem so overwhelming that dropping out of the effort seems easier. My small effort is hardly going to make any difference.

But that is just the point of this story. One person didn't meet all the needs that came about post Black Saturday, but thousands of people, who gave what they could, formed an army of responders. These people were the ones who gave material goods, who gave time and effort, who gave space, who gave a listening ear—this army was the answer to the desperate cry for help.

We live in a society where the humanist philosophy of individualism is becoming increasingly dominant as the foundation from which we make decisions. Lois Tverberg describes our western culture with the acronym WEIRD—Western, Educated, Industrialised, Rich, Democratic. She goes on to say that '...we place a strong emphasis on individualism and independence [defining] ourselves in terms of our rights and freedoms'.[2] Much of the non-western world don't see personal autonomy as important, but see people as members of community, whether it be family, tribe or nation.

During the Black Saturday crisis, Australians reached into that community spirit and banded together. On the whole, it brought out the best in people when they realised that their community was hurting, and so they were hurting too. They did not see how the situation might be affecting them personally, but saw how the situation was affecting the whole. As a result, what they gave, they gave for the good of the whole. The response was not motivated by how this would benefit the individual. As John said, there was no evidence of anyone trying to use the situation to gain power and position. The aid effort was not coming from an individual or independent perspective. It was coming from what was best for the community— for others.

---

2. Tverberg, L., (2018) *Reading the Bible with Rabbi Jesus: How a Jewish Perspective Can transform Your Understanding.*, Baker Books: Ada.

Australians pride themselves on their 'looking-out-for-their-mates' attitude, and we do see that come forward in times of national crisis. But sadly, once the story disappears from the headlines, we are being influenced by the 'what's-best-for-me' individualism attitude. It is becoming easier to dismiss the chronic crises that exist in our community. I'm ashamed to admit that I have learned to walk past a homeless person and not let that person's plight bother me too much. I have learned to hear about the lonely, the struggling, the refugee and not lose any sleep over it.

I am not advocating we spend sleepless nights troubled over the problems of the whole world that we cannot change, but I believe the purpose of this story is to inspire us to look for a situation where we can make a difference. We can give time, money, interest, and when pooled together with many others who also give what they can, the community spirit begins to push back against the overwhelming need.

John and Jan are Christian people, who are motivated not only by compassion and community spirit, but also by faith. It has already been established that it is not just Christians who have compassion and are prepared to give in times of need, but if you are a Christian, I would like to discuss something that is important for you to keep in mind.

In Matthew 25:31-46, Jesus talks about that day when he returns and sets up his kingdom. He describes how he will separate people as one would separate sheep and goats. To the ones on his right, he gives the following commendation:

> *For I was hungry and you gave me something to eat,*
> *I was thirsty and you gave me something to drink, I*
> *was a stranger and you invited me in, I needed clothes*
> *and you clothed me, I was sick and you looked after*
> *me, I was in prison and you came to visit me. (NIV)*

If you recall this story, you will know that those he was calling to move into their inheritance in the kingdom were confused. They did not recall having ever done any of these things to Jesus. He tells them that on every occasion they did something for the least of these, they did something for him.

Sobering as that part of the story is, it gets more tense.

He then talks to those who were on his left and tells them they are cursed to the eternal fires reserved for the devil and his angels. This is serious business. Of all the references where the word hell has been the translation from the original language, this is one of the very few where Jesus means the eternal fires of damnation. Other hell translations (Sheol, Gehenna) refer to the grave and the rubbish dump outside of Jerusalem, but this one, he means hell, as we understand it. And it isn't the thief, the murderer or the sexually immoral he is talking to. He is addressing those who have withheld aid and care from those in need.

Earlier in Matthew 7, Jesus was talking to a group of religious enthusiasts who have prophesied, cast out demons and performed miracles all in his name. Yet he tells them, 'I never knew you'. They were shocked, having called him Lord, but he clarifies that the ones he knows are the ones who did the will of the Father. When we boil it down, apparently prophesying and miracle working do not count as the hallmarks of the will of the Father.

What is the will of the Father? Well, I believe you will find consistently, throughout the Bible, Old and New Testament, that being kind and generous is associated with being righteous. Take a look at this Old Testament scripture:

Isaiah 58:2-10 (NIV)

For day after day they seek me out; they seem eager to know my ways, as if they were a nation that does what is right and has not forsaken the commands of its God...'Why have we fasted,' they say, 'and you have not seen it? Why have we humbled ourselves, and you have not noticed?'

> *Yet on the day of your fasting, you do as you please and exploit all your workers. Your fasting ends in quarrelling and strife, and in striking each other with wicked fists. You cannot fast as you do today and expect your voice to be heard on high. Is this the kind of fast I have chosen, only a day for people to humble themselves?*
>
> *Is that what you call a fast, a day acceptable to the Lord?*
>
> *Is not this the kind of fasting I have chosen: to loose the chains of injustice and untie the cords of the yoke, to set the oppressed free and break every yoke? Is it not to share your food with the hungry and to provide the poor wanderer with shelter—when you see the naked, to clothe them, and not to turn away from your own flesh and blood? Then your righteousness will go before you...Then you will call, and the Lord will answer...*
>
> *If you do away with the yoke of oppression, with the pointing finger and malicious talk, and if you spend yourselves in behalf of the hungry and satisfy the needs of the oppressed, then your light will rise in the darkness, and your night will become like the noonday.*

It is a long scripture to read but read it again. This is consistent with what Jesus has said in Matthew. The Lord has made it quite clear what he expects of us. Individualism and taking care of my own needs and wants may be the mantra of the society we live in, but it does not always reflect the heart of our Father. Jesus places high value on the work that meets the needs of the hungry and oppressed.

This heart of generosity is something that does not always come naturally. In our current WEIRD society we have advertising images pushed at us constantly through every device and media outlet, tantalising us with ideas of pleasure, leisure and personal fulfilment. It is hard not to turn our hearts in that direction. Even with the advertising from charity organisations, we can still bypass those needs and put them off for another time.

My challenge is to make a deliberate decision to stop and hear the cry of those in pain—those who are homeless, hungry, hurting. I can't do it all, but I can do something. And I need to become aware of the hell on my doorstep, and of the agencies who are there on the frontlines trying desperately to meet the needs. This is the heart of the God I serve, and I need to listen to His heart.

In the following chapter, we have assembled information about a number of agencies who are connecting with the least of these. I strongly encourage you to look through the list, read some of the testimonies and see if there is one that is near you who is looking for the type of help you have to offer.

God Bless you in your endeavours.

CHAPTER TEN
How To Become A Part Of The Support Network

A Resource Appendix

While this book is based on our ministry experience in Melbourne, Victoria, Australia, and we have been working with local support services, we do not want to ignore other national and international organisations worthy of financial and hands-on support. Hence, we have included some mainstream websites for national and international organisations.

We suggest you consider where your heart leads you and research the following options by going online through the link/s provided. These websites present a gateway into various different spheres of support that reach beyond your situation.

Don't forget to check with your local church to see if they run a food bank, charity shop, or community support group. Typically, most churches support initiatives run with the aid of volunteers, and even if you don't attend that church, they will likely welcome your offer of support.

This could be the beginning of a very exciting and worthwhile journey for you and/or your friends and family, helping to link arms with those less fortunate than you, and join forces with others who have a similar passion.

One local charity agency we have personal connection with is a group called Open House. The CEO, Paul Burgess, has kindly provided a description of the work they do and a short testimonial.

Open House

https://www.openhousecic.org.au/#/

Tackling social isolation head-on through creative programs and activities for all ages, giving people a place to belong since 1971.

We have programs and activities for anyone and everyone who is lonely or socially isolated.

Social isolation is a debilitating situation for anyone. It affects people of all ages and backgrounds.

Our Mission

- To live out Matthew 25:34-40 and Matthew 28:18-20
- To give long-term friendship and support to children, young people and adults in our community, particularly those who are disadvantaged or socially isolated.
- To provide a place with a relaxed environment where people are welcomed, encouraged to feel they belong, are cared for and supported.
- To give opportunities for people to express themselves and encouragement for those who wish to make positive changes to their lives.

Our Values

- We respect each person, their social, racial and religious beliefs, and treat them with dignity.
- We value each person as unique and loved by God.

- We value and freely offer friendship and support to those in need in our community in accordance with God's commands.
- We value, share with and support people unconditionally.

Testimonies

Nicholas (who is now eighteen years old) was referred to our Youth Workshop Mentoring Program (YWMP) from a local school. He had been disengaging from school and had an interest in woodwork. Initially he was shy with low self-esteem. As Nicholas continued to attend the YWMP he began to share a little about himself and his self-confidence grew. In the workshop, he enjoyed working with wood, and the desire to be a carpenter started to grow. We helped Nicholas connect with the school coordinator, who identified a pre-apprenticeship course. With this course as a goal, Nicholas found motivation to attend school regularly. We saw an opportunity to employ him for two days a week as a Property Maintenance Trainee. Today Nicholas is thriving in his new role. His confidence and skills continue to improve with each passing week.

One Voice

Another group we support and have had personal contact with, is the One Voice group, founded by Josh Wilkins.

Our Vision – restoring dignity and hope, one life at a time.
https://onevoice.org.au/

The One Voice group work with homeless people in various cities around Australia, providing facilities to shower and wash clothes. Toiletries are provided along with food and an opportunity to sit and talk. The following short story tells of one young lady whose life has been restored through the support of this group.

Josh Wilkins, founding director of One Voice, met seventeen-year-old Maryane when he strategically spent six months living on the streets of Melbourne. As Josh immersed himself in the raw reality of the city's homelessness crisis, he found Maryane sleeping under a railway bridge. Since meeting Josh and the One Voice team, and with their support, Maryane has been restored back to her family. Now twenty-two, Maryane has successfully completed two diplomas in Drug and Alcohol counselling and a Certificate IV in Community Services.

We look forward to opening our restoration and housing facility—Elevate—with Maryane, where she will use her education to support the restoration of many other young people.

Rahab Ministries

We have had direct contact with several people who have worked with this support group. Rahab Ministries are found in cities around Australia. This short information package was provided by Ruthie Byrne, Victorian coordinator of Rahab Ministries.

Rahab is a ministry to those who feel trapped in the sex industry.

> 'Every job I do I die inside.' - Australian sex worker

> 'I was happy doing this at the beginning because of the money, but after one year, I feel my soul has gone.' - Korean sex worker.

These two comments are indicative of the things we commonly hear from the women when we visit the brothels every month.

Rahab statistics say that 92% of the women working as sex workers want to leave the sex industry.

The girls may be trapped because of debt, poverty, addictions, pimps, bad partners etc.

Rahab has been able to offer support to women in the industry by giving free English lessons, counselling, therapy, friendships, coffee catch-ups, legal advice, prayer and referrals so that women can retrain for another career. Often, unfortunately, the post-traumatic stress they have experienced, even after being in the sex industry for as little as a year, is enough to emotionally and mentally cripple them, making a nine-to-five type job difficult. Even participating in further training is hard, and taking the risk to trust those around them to simply relate on a professional level, can be a tremendous strain. Rahab seeks to walk with women through this process to ensure they reach a place of wholeness.

The woman who founded Rahab ministries in 2003 had been working in Cambodia with the women and children trapped in the sex industry. When she returned to Adelaide, she felt a strong call to work with the women in Adelaide who felt caught in the sex industry, and hence the Rahab Ministry was established. Rahab seeks to offer them an opportunity to meet with Jesus, and help them come to a place of peace and wholeness within themselves.

Rahab provides extensive training to equip Christian women to set up teams and to reach the women in the brothels and massage parlours, strip clubs, motels, hotels and the women who work on the streets. If you are someone who prays, does craft, bakes, teaches English, or if you feel called to work as an outreach or pastoral care volunteer, there is work that you can do.

Rahab now has sixteen trained teams throughout Australia.

If you would like to know more about Rahab go to:
www.rahab.com.au
Victorian Branch - westvic.rahab@gmail.com

Other support agencies include:
- **World Vision** – https://www.worldvision.com.au/
- **Red Cross** – https://www.redcross.org.au/
- **Salvation Army** – http://www.salvationarmy.org.au/en/Find-Us/Victoria/CrisisServices/
- **City of Melbourne** – Helping out Booklet https://www.melbourne.vic.gov.au/sitecollectiondocuments/helping-out-booklet-map.pdf
- **Rosies – Friends on the Street** – Outreach to marginalised people http://rosies.org.au/ Situated throughout Queensland
- **The Pyjama Foundation** – Helping foster kids with reading and other learning activities https://thepyjamafoundation.com/ Available in QLD, NSW and Victoria

One Final Word
Meredith

The words that prompted me to pursue this project were 'messy church'.

In our final discussions Jan said to me that she was concerned that people might read this book, close it and forget. We pray that some readers will have been moved by God to pursue action.

John, Jan and myself have all been brought up in church culture, and each of us are aware that the various churches we have been in over the years have, on the whole, been neat and tidy and ordered. That's not necessarily bad, but it is a rare occasion that someone who is truly messed up will walk in, and if they do, they don't often stay. There are a few churches whose pastoral team has a strong conviction to make their church halls open to everyone, in whatever state and condition, and they usually present an eclectic group. Churches who have boldly taken on this call take the good, the bad and the ugly, and grapple with all the challenges that this kind of congregation brings.

Our challenge, if we live in comfy Christian-land, is how to do as Jesus has asked us. This book is not meant as a tool for folks to take to their pastors, to browbeat them into changing the way their congregations work. But we do hope this book is an encouragement to individuals, both within your particular church organisation and other organisations that focus on specific needs in the community. Perhaps your church has the capacity to do something and may already be active. Perhaps you can encourage this work, or look outside the walls of your church building, and connect with an organisation that is set up to deal with the different needs that present in our society.

An important thing to remember is that you can't do it all, and you do have to count the cost. But in all honesty, most of us could do something. If you don't have extra money, but you have extra time, then find a group and volunteer your time. If you don't have time, but you have money, make sure you go above and beyond with your giving. Make the finances available to these groups so they can continue to function effectively.

There was one other area that Jan highlighted. She has always wondered what might have been different if they'd had the personnel who were prepared to be committed to serious prayer. Do you believe in the power of prayer? Does it make a difference? From my experience, I believe it does, and what you have to give may come in the form of a commitment to pray. Prayer for the leaders and workers, prayer for the clients—those who are broken or hurting in some way. And most importantly, prayer that the love of God would not just be shared in a practical way, but that the Spirit of God would draw many to that place of relationship with him.

About the Authors

Based in Melbourne, Australia, **John and Jan Graham** have worked in Christian ministry for 25 years in various capacities of pastoral care. Both have a strong passion for the link between church and community. John and Jan have been married for 34 years and have two married children, and a dog.

They currently work as care pastors with Hope Centre, Bundoora http://www.hopecentrebundoora.com.au/

South Australian Author, **Meredith Resce**, has been writing since 1991, and has had books in the Australian market since 1997.

Following the Australian success of her *'Heart of Green Valley'* novel series, they were released in the UK and USA.

'Hell on the Doorstep' is Meredith's 19th published project, the second non-fiction.

Apart from writing, Meredith also takes the opportunity to speak to groups on issues relevant to relationships and emotional and spiritual growth.

Meredith has also been co-writer and co-producer in the 2007 feature film production, *'Twin Rivers'*.

With her husband, Nick, Meredith has worked in Christian ministry since 1983.

Meredith and Nick have three adult children, one daughter and two sons.

www.meredithresce.com
www.facebook.com/MeredithResceAuthor

www.ingramcontent.com/pod-product-compliance
Lightning Source LLC
Chambersburg PA
CBHW070437010526
44118CB00014B/2084